CREDO

Faith and Philosophy
in Contemporary Ireland

Edited by Stephen J. Costello

The Liffey Press

≈the
liffey
press

Published by
The Liffey Press Ltd
Ashbrook House, 10 Main Street
Raheny, Dublin 5, Ireland
www.theliffeypress.com

A catalogue record of this book is
available from the British Library.

ISBN 1-904148-30-1

Printed in the Republic of Ireland by Colour Books Ltd.

CONTENTS

Acknowledgements

I would like to extend my huge and heartfelt gratitude to the contributors in this book: Ger Casey, Hugh Cummins, Mitch Elliott, Richard Kearney, Cathy Molloy, Ellen O'Malley-Dunlop, Pat Treacy and Paddy Quinn. They gave of their time and energy and without them this book would simply not have been written.

My profuse thanks also to my family, especially my parents, Val and Johnny, for their encouragement, interest and inestimable support.

To all my friends for their comforting and much-needed presence in my life, especially John Rice and Darren Cleary.

John is a rock of support and always gives good, sound advice; his optimism and encouraging nature have energised me. Thank you John for your years of supportive friendship.

I have had the sheer pleasure and privilege of Darren's company, with whom I have enjoyed intense and the deepest of one-on-one conversations, usually once or twice a week privately in some pub. You enliven my soul Darren and your friendship means more to me than you will ever know.

To Mark and Kelly Coyle, Thomas O'Connor, Oisín and Elva Quinn, Alan Dodd, Brigid Ruane, Brendan Dowling, Mészáros István, Fr Terence Hartley, Bob Haugh, Fr Derek Smyth, Ronan Sheehan, Luke Sheehan and Fr John Harris. I realise that all of you have, at different times, enjoyed as well as endured me. I am only too aware of my faults as a friend and of your patience, understanding and love. I am eternally grateful.

You should all know that your friendships mean the world to me.

Dedication

I dedicate this book to Patrick Treacy and
Linda Rainsberry. May the One remain the
centre of all attraction for you both — always.

ABOUT THE CONTRIBUTORS

Stephen J. Costello, Editor

Born in Dublin, educated at St Gerard's School and Castleknock College, Stephen J. Costello studied philosophy at University College Dublin, gaining an MA and PhD and subsequently trained as a psychoanalyst. He is a lecturer in Philosophy and Psychoanalysis at the DBS School of Arts. Dr Costello is a member of the Association for Psychoanalysis and Psychotherapy in Ireland and also of The Irish Aikido Association. He is the author of *Basil Hume* (Veritas, 1988), *The Irish Soul: In Dialogue* (The Liffey Press, Dublin, 2001) and *The Pale Criminal: Psychoanalytic Perspectives* (Karnac, London and New York, 2002). He edited *The Search for Spirituality: Seven Paths within the Catholic Tradition* (The Liffey Press, Dublin, 2002) and is the author of a forthcoming book on the philosophy of happiness.

Gerard Casey

Born in Cork in 1951, educated at the Presentation Brothers College, after working abroad for some years, Gerard Casey returned to Ireland to take his primary degree in philosophy at University College Cork in 1978. He studied in Notre Dame from 1978-1983, gaining an MA and PhD. He taught in the School of Philosophy at The Catholic University of America from 1983 to 1986 and has been on the staff of the Philosophy Department at University College Dublin since 1986. He gained his LLB degree from the University of London in 2001 and is presently working on his LLM in UCD. Currently, Dr Casey is Head of the Philosophy Department at UCD.

Hugh Cummins

Hugh Cummins holds a BA in Philosophy from the Milltown Institute of Theology and Philosophy and an MPhil in Psychoanalytic Studies from Trinity College Dublin. He currently works in a homeless night shelter for the Catholic Social Services Agency, Crosscare.

Mitch Elliott

Mitch Elliott interrupted his scientifically oriented education in the US to complete his military service, then completed two degrees in Paris. The primary one (*Licence-ès-Lettres*) was in history, human geography, and German studies, whilst the secondary one was in maths and physics. In a parallel manner, his first career was in electronic engineering (metrology), yet during that time he was preparing for a second career by studying psychoanalysis. He is now a psychoanalyst in private practice, working mainly in Dublin, but having a smaller practice in Belfast. He is a founder member and director of the Irish Institute for Psycho-Social Studies (IIPSS) and is the fourth president of the Irish Psycho-Analytical Association, founded in 1942.

Richard Kearney

Richard Kearney holds the Charles B. Seelig Chair in Philosophy at Boston College. The author of more than twenty books on philosophy, politics and culture, including *The Wake of Imagination* (1988), *Poetics of Modernity* (1998), *Postnationalist Ireland* (1997) and *States of Mind* (1995), Professor Kearney has also published two novels that have been translated into various European languages and a volume of poetry. He has served as a member of the Irish Arts Council and the Higher Education Authority. He is currently Chairman of the Film Studies School at University College Dublin and a member of the Royal Irish Academy. His most recent philosophical trilogy consists of: *On Stories* (Routledge, 2001); *The God Who May Be* (Indiana University Press, 2001); and *Strangers, Gods and Monsters: Ideas of Otherness* (Routledge, 2002).

Cathy Molloy

Cathy Molloy was formerly an associate lecturer in theology at The Milltown Institute of Theology and Philosophy. She is presently working as a researcher at the Jesuit Centre for Faith and Justice in Dublin. She is the author of *Marriage: Theology and Reality* (Columba Novalis, 1996) and recently edited and co-authored *Windows on Social Spirituality* (Columba, 2003), a publication of the Jesuit Centre for Faith and Justice.

Ellen O'Malley-Dunlop

Ellen O'Malley-Dunlop works as a psychotherapist and group analyst. She is a founder member of the Irish Institute for Psychoanalytic Psychotherapy and was Chairperson of the Irish Council for Psychotherapy (1999–2001). She is currently completing her MLitt in Irish Folklore at UCD. She is former Chieftain of the O'Malley Clan.

Patrick Quinn

Patrick Quinn was educated in University College Dublin and the University of Liverpool. He is Head of the Philosophy Department at All Hallows College Dublin and also lectures philosophy in University College Dublin, Dublin City University and Dublin Business School. He is the author of *Aquinas, Platonism and the Knowledge of God* (Avebury, Guildford, 1996) and has contributed to other books and journals on philosophy and education. Dr Quinn also works in careers guidance and counselling.

Patrick Treacy

Patrick Treacy lives with his wife Linda Rainsberry and their three children, Sophia, Samuel and Joshua at Ennisnag, Stoneyford, County Kilkenny. At this location, they are involved in a venture entitled Integritas, which is seeking to develop an integral vision and practice of the Christian faith. This aspiration is broadly outlined in his contribution to this present publication. Patrick Treacy also practices as a barrister-at-law on the South Eastern Circuit of Ireland.

PREFACE

Traditionally, philosophy has been conceived as providing a propaedeutic to (Catholic) theology; philosophy as the hand-maid and ancillary of theology. But the relationship between reason and revelation is problematic; it is replete with rifts, rup-tures, fissures. On the one hand, there are the Thomists and Natural Theologians who argue that the existence of God can be proved philosophically, by the natural operation of the hu-man intellect. They do not reject faith though. It is a question of faith *and* reason, of *fides et ratio*. On the other hand, there are the fideists who believe that to assent to God's existence in-volves a crucifixion of the understanding — one must commit suicide with reason. They jettison and reject reason. The case is one of *credo quia absurdum* or *credo quia intelligiam*.

This book revolves around this dialectic. Not, "I believe be-cause it is absurd" or "I believe because it is intelligible" but this: "I believe in order to understand but also I understand in order to believe". Such is the hermeneutic circle. I am increas-ingly aware that I am not up to the task of being a Christian but I take comfort from Kierkegaard's remark that when we die we won't be asked why we didn't live more like Christ but why we didn't live more like ourselves. I trust and have faith in the Ab-solutely First and Last Reality. My belief is haunted by unbelief, as is proper, or else I would be certain and only the psychotic is that. We cannot know for certain but faith must be reasonable. I am on the side of those agonised Christians — Pascal, Una-muno, Dostoyevsky, Simone Weil and of those tragic religion-ists like Camus and Freud, Iris Murdoch and Wittgenstein — good people all.

The idea for this present book came after the favourable response to my first book, *The Irish Soul: In Dialogue*. Shortly after its publication I was interviewed on the radio by Marian Finucane and subsequently by the Jesuits, which resulted in a second interview for a CD with the title "No Simple Faith". I was then asked to pen a short summary of my Christian faith for a Jesuit website, "Catholic Ireland". All this concentrated my mind and made me focus on what I really believe. I mentioned all this to a friend who decided, for purely personal reasons of his own, to write down his own thoughts on the subject. The idea for this project was consolidated amid subsequent conversations and my friend's essay is included in this compilation.

This book is a collection of diverse points of view. The contributors themselves come from different professions that include philosophy, theology, psychotherapy and law. I asked people for whom the God question was alive and burning. I wanted theists and asked them to reflect on their faith and write something personal without necessarily being intimate or confessional. These articles are personal testimonies, *apologias* of the Christian faith. The book is on faith and philosophy in the context of the contemporary cultural climate of the Republic of Ireland at the beginning of the twenty-first century. I think the book nicely complements both *The Irish Soul* and a book I edited entitled *The Search for Spirituality: Seven Paths Within the Catholic Tradition*, both also published by The Liffey Press.

Within the covers of these pages you will encounter men and women who are searching, searching still and questioning. They are not smug or superior, simply wondering at the meaning of it all, and sometimes marvelling, but also despairing, for faith is not easy. It exacts a burden. Atheists are people who *believe* that there is no God and the consequences of both theism and of atheism are equally inescapable and perhaps all-consuming. The people here have all struggled and experienced both faith and failure, consolation and desolation, God hidden and revealed, lost and found again . . . and lost again in a never-ending cycle of hope and despair, light and darkness. These pages tell of *faith in search of understanding*.

Chapter 1

FAITH IN SEARCH OF UNDERSTANDING

Gerard Casey

I

From the age of about fourteen my religious faith was marked by increasing intensity, a common enough teenage experience. At the same time, however, I was coming to have doubts, doubts that I found difficult to express since I didn't possess the requisite vocabulary or ideas, nor did I have those around me with whom I could discuss such matters. When I was sixteen I discovered Bertrand Russell's *Why I'm not a Christian*. On reading this book all the inchoate questions I had suddenly became clear. Russell's book acted like sulphuric acid on the grounds of my faith; I found that they could not stand up to rational criticism so I abandoned my faith and, for the next fourteen years or so, I was a convinced atheist — an atheist, note, not an agnostic for I subscribed to the principle that if there was no evidence for a belief system then that constituted evidence for its negation.

I continued my study of philosophy, first independently and then at university, and eventually found myself, at the age of twenty-nine, a graduate student at the University of Notre Dame. Many of my fellow graduate students in philosophy were Christians of one sort of another, mostly Protestant, from an astonishing variety of backgrounds — Dutch Calvinist, Wesleyan Methodist, Southern Baptist. Despite these differences they were all firm believers. That came as a shock to me. Here were people who, according to the normal indicators, appeared to be intelligent but yet they believed in God. Many of them were researching in the area of the Philosophy of Religion so I often found myself drawn into conversations on religious topics. Sometimes the talk would be directed to questions about the actual content of faith of different Christian denominations. While my fellow students often disagreed among themselves, they generally congratulated themselves on at least not holding the indefensible beliefs of Catholics. Now I didn't mind the Church being hanged but my innate sense of justice demanded that she be hanged for the right offence and it often seemed to me that the accusations that were levelled against her were simply wrong. The accusations might be, for example, that Catholics had a mechanical "filling station" theory of grace — that all you had to do was to turn up to the filling station (i.e. Church) on a Sunday and stock up on grace for the next week; or that according to Catholic doctrine your salvation was a matter that could be arranged entirely by yourself — a long list of good deeds obliging God, as it were, to award you salvation. Now all I had in my head from my own religious education were the shreds and patches of my knowledge of the elementary catechism and from this I was able to draw some bits and pieces according to need. I found myself thrust into the role of defender of the faith in spite of myself, often having to flee to the library stacks to sustain the role. This went on for almost three years so that I came to know a lot of Catholic doctrine in a detached fashion, as one might come to know the doctrines of Buddhism or Confucianism.

By now I was married and my wife and I had one child. Having a child makes you take the long view of things. When you are single your horizon of concern extends perhaps a few weeks into the future; when you have a child, your horizon shoots out about 20 years. Slowly but surely topics that had not been, to use William James's words, "live options" for me for many years now became live again. I still didn't quite know what I thought about all this religion, but I was definitely in a state of change. My atheistic certainties had been shaken. Where I would end up I didn't know. I was impressed with the intellectual coherence and rigour of Catholic doctrine; accept the starting points and everything else had a ring of coherence and consistency and a certain kind of inevitability that was nonetheless unpredictable. I stayed in this state of detached conviction for some time. Then, one day, on my way home from lectures, I was passing by the Sacred Heart Church in Notre Dame. Skirting around the back I was about to pass the entrance to the crypt chapel when I felt a strong impulse to go in. I did. A confession box was operational and without pausing to reflect I went straight in and made my first confession for almost fourteen years. Afterwards I was quite surprised by what I had done. Looked at providentially, my fourteen years in the desert of unbelief led to my being rationally persuaded of the truth and beauty of the faith before I gave it my real assent. Since then my faith has never wavered though I often have had what Douglas Adams called "a long dark tea-time of the soul". Having, as it were, been on the other side of the fence, it no longer has any attractions for me.

II

Faith's search for understanding is often presented as if it were a phenomenon that occurs only in a religious context. I believe, however, that it is a general condition of the pursuit of all knowledge. To think that we can have knowledge without faith is to take the road that eventually leads to scepticism. Scepticism prizes cleanliness over disorder, form over content, sterility over fertility and certainty over doubt. In the interests of intellectual hygiene, nothing is admitted into one's mind until it has been inspected and passed free of all infectious diseases. But taken to its logical conclusion this attitude won't allow us to pass *anything* fit for consumption — for what is it that is going to do the inspecting in the first place and why should *it* be presumed to be uncontaminated? There is no antiseptically sterile Archimedean point on which we can stand prior to our engagement with the world; Descartes gallantly attempted to discover such a point and Descartes failed. As we now look back on the philosophy in the twentieth century we may reflect that if it has taught us anything surely it is that we are thoroughly engaged with our world even before the beginning of inquiry and that our efforts at understanding and clarification have to be conducted from a position of prior engagement. It's like living in a house while you redecorate it. It would certainly be a lot easier to move out and live somewhere else while all the fuss is going on but if you can't do this, as you can't with your beliefs, you have to live with the mess.

For a long time I have suspected that there is something intellectually immature about scepticism. It is, I believe, often the result of a failed search for certainty. When knowledge and certainty are effectively equated then failure to achieve certainty almost invariably leads to scepticism. The mature inquirer will demand and accept from each area of inquiry that level of knowledge that it will sustain. As Aristotle said long ago in the *Nicomachean Ethics*:

> . . . it is the mark of an educated man to look for precision in each class of things just so far as the nature of the subject admits; it is evidently equally foolish to accept probable reasoning from a mathematician and to demand from a rhetorician scientific proofs. It is as absurd to accept probabilities from a mathematician as it is to demand certainty from morals. (Book I, Chapter 3)

It doesn't follow from this that one's initial positions are incapable of changing, even of being abandoned. It may be that the process of seeking understanding leads precisely to the abandonment of our initial position and to the assumption of another. It may be that at the end of our inquiry we come around again to our point of departure albeit at a higher level. Whether or which, the point is that there is no uncontaminated, no value-free or uncommitted starting point.

One of Wittgenstein's targets in *On Certainty* is the notion of hyperbolic doubt, which is a staple dialectical device of scepticism. An all-too-easy assumption of the sceptic is that in relation to any position whatsoever one may always and everywhere express doubts. But, as Wittgenstein puts it, "doubt needs grounds". The position of the sceptic who reiterates, "And why should we accept that?" is very like that of the child who has learnt the power of the question "Why?" to elicit a response from its distracted parents.

Wittgenstein's position is not a foundationalism in any recognisably standard version; he does not hold that there are propositions that are self-evident, obviously true, or that manifest any other variety of intrinsic epistemological specialness — it is simply that in any complex of beliefs and practices some are at any given time more central to the complex as a whole, and thus more resistant to change, than others. But these propositions do not necessarily maintain that functionally privileged position over time. Wittgenstein uses a striking image of the interaction between a river and its bed to illustrate the thesis that systems of beliefs are internally dynamic and are also in continual interaction with other systems of belief. Relative to the water in the river, the bed of the river is stable and abiding. But the river bed exists as such only because it has been carved out by the waters that previously ran in it and because of the continuing action of the water the course of the riverbed can be, and sometimes is, changed.

In the religious context, then, to seek an understanding of one's faith is simply to do what all seekers after knowledge do. It is not necessarily to prejudge the questions of whether or to what extent the content of one's faith is rational. It may be that all that one can arrive at is a rational articulation of a content that, in the end, cannot be rationally justified but then, as Wittgenstein remarks, enquiry has to end somewhere — why not here?

Sometimes believers are challenged by non-believers to prove their beliefs. Failure to deliver such proof is then taken to be tantamount to disproof. Perhaps it might be worthwhile to examine the concept of proof. The first thing to realise is that all proof is relative. Anything at all can be proved provided that one has been equipped with the right starting points. And that, of course, is the rub. Here, for example, is a snappy six-line proof for the existence of God:

Where υ = "It is possible that..."; or "possibly": v = "It is necessary that..."; or "necessarily"; and G = God exists, then

    1. υG *[It is possible that God exists]*
    2. $G \: \Pi \: vG$ *[If God exists, then God necessarily exists]*

3.   ʊG ⊓ ʊνG [if it is possible that God exists, then it is possible that God necessarily exists]

4.   ʊνG [It is possible that God necessarily exists]

5.   νG [God necessarily exists]

6.   G [God exists]

This looks as if it were a latter-day equivalent of the "proof" given by a famous French mathematician — La Place, I think — to the assembled Russian nobles "x + y = z, therefore, God exists". Without wishing to deny that logic can be used for the purposes of intellectual intimidation, this proof is not quite in the same category of disreputability as the La Placean one. The two premises are not implausible. The first states that it is possible that God exists. Unless you are a necessitarian atheist this would seem to be true. (A necessitarian atheist holds not just that God *does not* exist; he holds that God *cannot* exist, a much stronger position.) The second premise fleshes out the content of an understanding of what orthodox theists, Christian, Jewish or Muslim, mean by God. For someone to be God is for that person to be an entity strictly incommensurate with the other things in this world. All the theistic religions believe that their God is transcendent; that the world is his creation and that he is not to be confused with anything in that world or with that world as a whole. Whatever or whether such a God may be, if he exists at all, then his existence is not contingent. The third step of the argument involves the application of an inference rule in one system of modal logic. The fourth step is simply a modal version of a common and uncontroversial inference rule in logic, *Modus Ponens*. Step five involves yet another inference rule from a system of modal logic; and the move from five to six is a basic insight of modal logic, namely, that it is valid to move from necessity to actuality.

Obviously, this argument is not beyond criticism; my point in putting it forward is precisely to make that point. While its premises are not implausible and its inferences not obviously wrong one may yet not feel rationally coerced by the argument even if one is unable to point to specific defects. Often, the demand made of the religious believer is often not just for a proof; it is for a proof that would be rationally coercive for all. But this is much too high a demand. It is a demand that if made in the science would invalidate scientific theories!

All proofs, then, are situated in a context, and it is only if the context is impeccable that the proof works without the possibility of a hitch. It is open to anyone who wishes to undermine your proof to broaden the context so that new questions are asked, new demands made for arguments, new demands made for evidence.

What this means is that it is perfectly possible to feel the probative force of an argument while another, equally rational person, does not. This experience is not confined to the world of religion; it happens all the time in politics, in sport and in art. Have we not all had the experience of believing a certain film to be brilliant, insightful, witty, enhanced by superlative acting and direction, deep and significant, only to find that someone close to us whose values and judgement we respect judges it to be superficial and trashy? The existence of a difference in judgement does not in itself necessarily lessen our attachment to our own judgement though subsequent discussion and reflection may do so. In most areas of life we do not require unanimity to justify our adoption of firm beliefs. It would be special pleading with a vengeance if it should be required in the case of religious beliefs.

One of the functions of faith's search for understanding is to open that faith out into new contexts, into new situations that it may not obviously cover. This is a risky venture for, as I indicated above, a consequence of this may be that you will find yourself forced to abandon your initial faith. But this is a risk that must be taken. As Thomas Kuhn has demonstrated so forcefully in his seminal work on the philosophy of science, such risk-taking does not require you to give up a position at the first sight of a difficulty (as Cardinal Newman said in a similar context, "Ten thousand difficulties do not make one doubt") but it does open up in principle the possibility of a renunciation of one's position if the difficulties should come to be experienced as insuperable.

What kinds of evidence might be germane to coming to or moving away from belief in a theistic God? Everything in the universe appears to be contingent, that is to say, there is nothing necessary about the existence of any particular thing. It exists now, it did not exist in the past, and it may not exist in the future. This contingency also seems to apply to the universe as a whole so that one does not necessarily commit the fallacy of composition if one concludes from the contingency of the parts to the contingency of the whole. So, if there is to be something rather than nothing, then the ground of that being must be sourced somewhere other than in any individual element of the universe or in the universe as a whole. There are, of course, many other features of the universe on which arguments for the existence of God can, and have, been based; change, causality, the phenomenon of order, conscience, etc.

On the negative side of the scale we have the problem of evil. The problem of evil takes its start from what would appear to be an obvious fact of human experience, namely, that there is evil, and quite a deal of it, in the world. Reading one of my favourite authors, Raymond Chandler, recently, I came across this passage in which our hero gathers his thoughts at the end of a very busy day at the office:

> When I got home I mixed a stiff one and stood by the open window in the living-room and sipped it and listened to the ground swell of the traffic on Laurel Canyon Boulevard and looked at the glare of the big, angry city hanging over the shoulder of the hills through which the boulevard had been cut. Far off the banshee wail of police or fire sirens rose and fell, never for very long completely silent. Twenty-four hours a day somebody is running, somebody else is trying to catch him. Out there in the night of a thousand crimes people were dying, being maimed, cut by flying glass, crushed against steering wheels or under heavy car tyres. People were being beaten, robbed, strangled, raped, and murdered. People were hungry, sick, bored, desperate with loneliness or remorse or fear, angry, cruel, feverish, shaken by sobs. (*The Long Good-Bye*, Chapter 38)

But it needs no ghost come from the grave to tell us this. Open the daily paper, for whom the maxim "no news is good news" might be more accurately converted to "no good news is news". Here we are presented with a diet not only of the human depravity that Chandler so graphically sketches, but of a host of fascinating natural disasters without notice of which we seem unable to enjoy our breakfast cereal, such as the devastation caused by earthquakes, floods, hurricanes, tornadoes, not to mention the less spectacular but even more relentless parade of the ills that human flesh is heir to — accident, illness, deformity and death. And while it may be hyperbolic to claim that we always and everywhere suffer pain, distress and misery there are few if any of us who have lived beyond childhood who have not experienced some serious degree of suffering.

The problem of evil arises when you put together the fact of human suffering with the notion of God that is common to the orthodox versions of the great theistic religions — Judaism, Christianity and Islam — from the apparently irreconcilable tensions generated by the clash between the fact of human suffering and the theistic conception of God as a Person possessed of certain hyperbolic characteristics or attributes, the Creator of the Universe and all it contains, and the Providential Guardian of that Universe.

Is this the last word? Of course not. One reply to the problem of evil could be that human choice is always made *sub ratione boni*, that is, under some aspect of goodness. At the moment of choice we choose what we choose because at that moment it appears to us as the most desirable among other goods. But what is good to us at any particular moment is not necessarily either the best, or even good at all *per se*. God wants us to choose Him but He will not coerce our choice. If our decision for or against God is to be real, God cannot reveal Himself to us as He is, otherwise there would simply be no contest; no created good could measure up to God. But *God cannot make us to be free and, at the same time, consistently override the consequences of our free choices whenever they result in evil*. To do so would be to refuse to take us seriously, to treat us as a father might when he "loses" a game of chess to his young child by deliberately blundering away his pieces; neither can God bring it about that *in our present circumstances*, in freely choosing, we choose only the good. Is *that* the last word? No — the process of argumentation is essentially dialectical, essentially open-ended.

III

In the last twenty years or so, we have witnessed a revolution in the position and status of the Catholic Church in Ireland. Much of the change has been a result of conditions that are more or less universal in the West; some are peculiar to Ireland. One of the most obvious and devastating factors that has contributed to the changing status of the Catholic Church has been the revelation of the existence and activities of priests who have sexually abused children and teenagers. While not all priests are child-abusers, nor is child abuse a phenomenon exclusively confined to the clergy, there is something particularly scandalous about the phenomenon of priests abusing young people. It is not only the abuse itself, which is obviously horrendous, but perhaps more so that such abuse should be perpetrated by those whose lives should be exemplary and who are accorded, or at least used to be accorded, so much respect and trust.

Almost as scandalous as the abuse itself has been the manner in which the Church has attempted to deal with the problem. In part this has resulted from the Church's acceptance of the secular doctrine of the "medicalisation of morality", the "it is not wrong but sick" school of thought. The Church should have known — none better — the difference between sin and sickness. Sickness is inadvertent and it excuses; sin is the result of a free choice and it must be repented. To conflate sickness and sin is to undermine human dignity by undermining human freedom. In the case of child abuse, the two concepts were conflated. Diabetes and pneumonia are illnesses; child abuse is a sin and a crime.

The root of the problem with clerical child abusers, as with all sinners, is that they did not make Christian choices, did not live their lives in fidelity to Christ's Church. They were not, nor are they, sick, unless we make the mistake of taking a metaphorical notion of sickness literally. The notion of sin, of transgressing God's laws, never a very popular notion needless to say, must return to the front of Catholic consciousness. This is not to point the finger at any particular person or group; we are all sinners — that much we do know for certain. But to deny the reality of sin is to make it all the more difficult to escape from its slavery; one might even speculate that this is the mysterious unforgivable sin against the Holy Spirit. Writing this on the first Sunday in Advent, I am reminded of one of today's Scriptural readings:

> O Lord, why dost thou make us err from thy ways
> And harden our heart, so that we fear thee not?
> In our sins we have been a long time, and shall we be saved?
> We have all become like one who is unclean
> And all our righteous deeds are like a polluted garment.
> We all fade like a leaf,
> And all our iniquities, like the wind, take us away.
> Thou hast hid thy face from us
> And hast delivered us into the hand of our iniquities. (Is 63:
>   17; 64: 5-7)

The Church is one, holy, catholic and apostolic; these are its essential marks. Its personnel, on the other hand, whether clerical or lay, are guaranteed neither unity, catholicity or holiness. We have need of all three, but of holiness I judge is our greatest need.

The news is not all bad. From my point of view the demise of the Catholic Church as a functional State Church is a matter of rejoicing. Unlike the situation in many European countries we have no official established church in this state. However, I think it would be true to say that that for a variety of historical and demographic reasons, the Catholic Church has functioned as a non-official established church. There are those who want to separate Church and State, largely for the purposes of, as they see it, freeing the State from Church interference. I would like to separate Church and State to free the Church from State interference. There is no reason, for example, why the Church should provide schools and schooling for the population at large. There is no reason why the Church should provide buildings and ceremonies for those who are not in any real sense its members. One may hope that an end is in sight to the baptising, communioning and confirming of the semi-pagan; the provision of churches for the wedding ceremonies of the non-practicing. It is time and beyond for the Church militant to be comprised of those who can actively and sincerely subscribe to its beliefs and practices, not those who are too intellectually slovenly to have the courage of their lack of convictions to leave. If the current crisis spells the end of the quasi-established Church and its associated cultural Catholics then it will have had an unintended benefit.

If the current crisis in the Church brings about an end to clericalism then another good will have come out of evil. I do not mean by clericalism the claim that there is a distinct clerical state with certain activities, for example, the celebration of the Eucharist, the hearing of confessions, and so on, being proper to that state. Clericalism is rather the improper attribution to or the claiming of special rights and privileges by those in the clerical state. In a curious way, some at least of those pushing for the ordination of women seem to be suffering from a kind of clericalism in that their understanding of what it is to be ordained seems to be centred on status and power rather than on service, on a view that to be a non-clerical Christian is somehow to be a Christian of a lower order.

Apart from the child abuse scandals, there are some other factors that contribute to the perception of crisis in the contemporary Church. One very important factor is the lack of clarity about what it is that a priest is supposed to be, a lack of clarity that affects not only laypeople but also priests themselves. Unsure of just what it is they are supposed to be doing and without the respect that was accorded to them in more innocent time many priests find themselves in situations not unlike that of the three stooges of Craggy Island. It is hardly surprising that, when what one has committed oneself to appears meaningless and is disvalued, there is a temptation to do nothing or to turn to other things.

There is often a lack of vertical or transcendent focus in the liturgy which is consequently reflected in belief and practice. Often the liturgy appears self-centred rather than God-centred. It seems to function as if it were some kind of social get together. As such it's pretty much a dismal failure. The Mass cannot compete in the entertainment value stakes with popular culture. It's bound to appear boring when compared to TV or film. But that is to confuse the ritual with the ephemeral, the mythic with the mundane. When understood as the reenactment of a cosmic drama there is nothing more gripping than the Mass.

There is, and has been for some time, a failure of nerve in religious instruction, reflecting an impatience with the necessity for intellectual distinctions, for definitions, for dogma. A generation, perhaps even two, have now left their Catholic schools with almost no knowledge of just what it is that their religion teaches. And ecumenism, which if it means not hitting your religious opponents over the head with a club and recognising that elements of truth can be found in more than one place is a commendable attitude, can sometimes lead to the belief that religious differences are insignificant, that they don't really matter at all. But this isn't ecumenism; it's indifferentism.

The solution to the Church's problems, *pace* its cultured despisers, is not to dispense with clerical celibacy, it isn't to admit women to the priesthood or to relax (as if it could) the moral law, particularly in relation to sexual morality. The reason these erstwhile solutions are not the answer is that this is not where the problem lies. Other Christian bodies have tried all these erstwhile solutions without any noticeable improvement in the behaviour of their members and leaders. The problems of the Church need to be seen in the larger national context where for some considerable time, as attested to by the proliferation of tribunals, many institutions have come under scrutiny: the beef industry, the blood transfusion service; the planning process; the gardaí. Moreover, the international context needs to frame the whole. Francis Fukuyama, commenting on the emergence of the information society, notes that "Hierarchies of all sorts, whether political or corporate, come under pressure and begin to crumble" and "Trust in many traditional types of authority, like politicians, police, and the military, has declined in most Western developed countries".[1] What he calls "The Great Disruption" (his term for post-1960s seriously deteriorating social conditions) has peaked in many other countries; it has still to reach its zenith in Ireland. But man cannot long tolerate the absence of order and meaning,[2] the need for which, if not as exigent as the need for food and drink, is every bit as important to human flourishing in the long run.

Notes

---

[1] Francis Fukuyama, *The Great Disruption* (1999, London: Profile Books), p. 4, 49.

[2] See Victor Frankl's *Man's Search for Meaning* (Washington Square Press).

Chapter 2

THE DESIRE OF THE GOD BEYOND GOD

Stephen J. Costello

> Where questions of religion are concerned people are guilty of every possible sort of dishonest and intellectual misdemeanour. Philosophers stretch the meaning of words until they retain scarcely anything of their original sense. They give the name "God" to some vague abstraction which they have created for themselves: having done so they can pose before all the world as deists, as believers in God, and they can even boast that they have recognized a higher, purer concept of God, notwithstanding that their God is now nothing more than an insubstantial shadow and no longer the mighty personality of religious doctrines — Freud, *The Future of an Illusion.*

Credo in unum deum. Ut deus vult. It is better to wait on God (*confere* Simone Weil) rather than to pray for Him (*pace* Emmanuel Levinas). Pray *to* Him but not *for* Him. God does not need us for Him to be fully God.

Can God's existence be proved philosophically? No, but it can be uncovered. Aquinas's five "proofs" convince only the theist. There must be a prior disposition. But there is another tradition in philosophy; there is Anselm, and the great Franciscans — Scotus and Bonaventure. The existential "certainty" of God's existence is rooted not in the *cogito* of pure reason but in the *credo* of the biblical message. Faith, however, is reasonable and must be shown to be thus. There are two errors: fideism and rationalism. I stand between Kantian rationalism and

Kierkegaardian fideism. There is an indissoluble unity between faith and reason — *fides et ratio*. Gnosticism is a heresy and is ubiquitous. It leads to the "immanentisation of the eschaton", to use Eric Voegelin's felicitous phrase.

A word on "certainty": we can never be *certain* that God exists. That would defeat the purpose. There is no such "consoling certainty of our Christian faith" as Pope John Paul II talks about. Faith is always haunted by unbelief and doubt and radical, haunting uncertainty. Christ on the Cross called out a lament at the loss of God. Dostoyevsky: "true faith comes from the crucible of doubt". As believers (not knowers) we must doubt daily. Perhaps prayer is a monologue of the deaf. Thus the difference between the philosopher and the theologian. Better to be a philosopher.

God's existence is not deductive nor can we rely exclusively on religious experience. There is no syllogism that proves God exists. There are experiential cues, though, that indicate the reasonableness of assent to the proposition "God exists", though the cues cannot compel the assent. There are tracks that lead to God — trinitarian traces. We have the codification of two thousand years of the experience of the Divine. The argument: the accumulation of various probabilities. There is evidence for the reasonableness of belief in God. There are experiential indicators, as we have said, that are theistically evidential. There are traces, which amount to a phenomenology of belief. Signposts abound suggesting an experiential confirmation.

It's a matter of *seeing*.

Kierkegaard felt that it was an impertinence to prove God's existence right under His very nose.

God does not have a shadow side as suggested by the Gnostic Jung.

Of course, God is not a man; "He" is trans-personal. In 1978 the Pope said that God is our father, but more, He is our mother. We must penetrate beyond image and idolatry.

Pascal's schism: the two gods — the God of the philosophers (the God of reason) and the God of Abraham, Isaac and Jacob (the God of revelation). The two must be conjoined. We need both faith and reason, Athens and Jerusalem. They are not pitted together in mortal combat, though they were for Unamuno.

Pascal's beautiful sentence: "the heart has its reasons of which reason knows nothing". It is the soul, rather than the speculative intelligence, that needs to believe, that longs for God and ultimate meaning and eternal hope and love. Faith is a refuge for anguish and torment. It is a "clearing", in the Heideggerian sense.

Contact with transcendence can soothe a man's soul. The choice is stark but simple: contemplate suicide and exit from the gross meaninglessness of an absurd life or go down on bended knee in worship before the God who made you. "Ponder on your bed and be still and know that I am God". It is a choice of closure (chaos) or of rediscovering the spiritual order of a meaningful existence in the cosmos. We are participants in the divine life.

God is Goal and Ground, the Beginning and the Beyond, Alpha and Omega. He is the One who unites and reconciles in sacred space. He is encountered in the hidden depths and dark recesses of the soul and in the cosmos. He is both immanent and transcendent. The pneumatic Centre draws us beyond. He is the source of all our eschatological expectations.

Desire springs from lack. We desire what we don't have. We desire God. The question is: does God desire us or is He as impassible as He is immutable? God does desire us but He desires us with a divine desire, with a desire that does not emanate from lack but from a source of superabundance and plenitude — one that overflows with love. He seeks us out and draws us to Him.

Did God create us because He needed us? Was He so alone in the vastness of that immense space that so terrified Pascal but that was such a comfort to Ortega? Is He not complete without us? God is self-sufficient.

God is present in us supernaturally, not naturally. That is why Meister Eckhart has been so sorely misinterpreted. Eckhart is a master of the spiritual life.

God consoles and deprives. There is the God of consolation and of desolation, of which St Ignatius speaks. It is important, though, to linger awhile in the void with its promise of nothingness or even to make the move that makes the void appear (*confere* Iris Murdoch). Life lessons may be learnt there.

God is infinite — infinite as in non-finite and *in* the finite, irreducible to intentionality. He is otherwise than being and beyond essence, other than otherwise (*confere* Levinas). Such alterity.

God is love — an arrow aflame with desire. The mystics burn with desire. And love crucified Love. All love ends on a cross, which is the ultimate symbol of love.

Why not do the *Spiritual Exercises*? — they are all about desire. Or practise the *Lectio Divina* and rest with the Word that was in the beginning? Ponder on the Psalms.

Life is meaningful only in so far as it culminates in death.

Death is not an event in life, however, as Wittgenstein tells us. We can't experience death though we will experience our dying to life and our rising again. What will be the words written of us in our obituaries, spoken of us at our funerals? The realisation that we are beings for death brings anxiety (*confere* Heidegger). There will always be at least one person who will be relieved that we have died. Hopefully.

The goal is not to aim to be holy — this can be a pious fraud. The aim is to be oneself and to be spent — to be contemplatives even in the midst of all activity. This is the aim of the Jesuits.

Religion must lead to transformation. A life must change. Wittgenstein thought one must amend one's ways and help others, though there is aggressivity present in the most Samaritan of aid (*confere* Jacques Lacan).

If faith is dead without good works so is faith worthless without justice.

Faith is a *passion* (Kierkegaard).

Iris Murdoch thought one must be good for nothing. I say: one must believe for nothing. This is the God beyond accusation and consolation, protection and punishment (*confere* Paul Ricoeur).

Christians are ill. We are sick, as both Kierkegaard and Nietzsche indicated.

We are ill at ease here. Our home is elsewhere. We are in exile — homeless.

The Fall is Real.

The truths of the Faith require, call out for, philosophical reflection.

Fall on your knees though they are stiff.

God, not Good (*à la* Iris Murdoch), is the magnetic centre towards which love naturally moves.

Do our lives and loves move God Himself to tears? Rilke wrote: "Who would hear me if I cried among the angelic order?" Do the angels hear our sighs, our cries, our songs of melancholy? Can our angels save us? I hear the beating of their wings, feel their breath over the deep.

There is a communion of the saints. The most recent member: St Padre Pio. They intercede; they do not intervene. God sings His holy songs through His saints.

Read Freud on religion. It is the greatest psychological critique ever penned. One's faith must be chastised, critiqued. If one's faith survives the critical chastisement from the Freudian hermeneutic then it is a surer, firmer faith, less idolatrous, no longer the bland, blind faith of the simple soul. If it doesn't survive it wasn't meant to survive. In my opinion, Freud was an "anonymous Christian", to use Karl Rahner's extraordinary (but problematic) expression. Freud did a great service to religious belief. Jung, the "believer", did a great disservice. Freud was an honest to God atheist. Ernst Bloch said he was an atheist for God's sake. Indeed.

We need Marx, Feuerbach, Nietzsche and Freud and their destructive critiques because a moment of destruction can lead to a new foundation and reconstruction and transcendence too.

Is there really no salvation outside Christ? "No one can come to the Father except through me." I cannot pronounce on this. But in my opinion, the truth subsists in the Catholic Church. Anglicans are Catholics.

Lacan said that the only atheists he ever met were those in the Vatican and that theologians, far more than anybody else, can do without God.

Most "atheists" are agnostics.

Philosophy is Socratic. Socrates said he didn't know everything. He knew he didn't know. Isn't that enough? Philosophy begins with ignorance and ends elsewhere. It begins in the classroom but may lead to a couch or a convent.

Philosophy lets the genie out of the bottle. Philosophy is not ideology or theology. It is a questioning and questing; it is a search, a lover's search for wisdom — one that can never be completely consummated. At the heart of philosophy is failure. Philosophers are failed lovers.

Philosophy is therapy and spiritual practice. Such was the ancient understanding of this name that never offends.

The question is everything but does it exist? The search itself is enough to fill a man's soul (*confere* Camus).

The mystery is that there is something not nothing (*confere* Leibniz and Heidegger). *That* the world is at all is the mystical (*confere* Wittgenstein).

Prayer? Sitting still, meditating, even drinking tea. It depends on how you drink it though.

Prayer is not the "flight of the alone to the Alone" (Plotinus). It is body and breath and rootedness. It is awareness and attention and seeing. Also sensing. It is hard to see what is under one's nose. If you want to hide a letter from prying eyes put it on the centre of the mantelpiece.

We do not pray; we are prayed.

We *share* in the divine life.

Nietzsche said there was only one Christian and He died on the Cross. Yes, but we can try. When Eric Voegelin, the philosopher, was asked whether he was a Christian, he replied: "I try to be."

Why try to mix together Eastern and Western spiritual practices into an eclectic mishmash? Don't you know that there is a contemplative tradition within Christianity? Nod over to the East but no need to go looking there.

There is no real Self, no Higher Self. There is no self at all. We are nothingness.

We are made to disappear. To be forgotten. Erased. Wiped out. Such is our privilege.

We are made of absence and God reveals Himself in His absence too — in footsteps on the sand, in a burning bush. God's trinitarian traces are everywhere evident in His creation.

We are stewards, not owners — of creation, of our bodies. Higher than apes but lower than angels.

(Cheerful) acceptance of creation not (weary) resignation. And love.

Is the theist happier so? No, not that. We cannot think that we are assured of Heaven. We are suspended between belief and unbelief. Theism and atheism are two sides of a Moebius strip, like happiness and unhappiness.

The true formula of atheism is not God is dead but God is unconscious. Truth leads to religion (*confere* Lacan).

The function of religious rites and prayer is to arouse the desire of God.

God is possible/actual/cannot not be, though we may not know it. Some people believe they do not believe.

Pascal: We would not have searched for God unless we had already found Him.

Augustine: Our hearts are restless. What do we love when we love our God?

Communion: the sacrament of love should be taken on one's tongue and kneeling. When the Mass was in Latin, at least people comprehended that it was the incomprehensible that was important.

The Spirit: a breath breathing in the dark.

The Spirit: dancing in my soul.

God is not dead, as Nietzsche thought, just eclipsed (*confere* Martin Buber).

In God, there is no why. He is simple and detached. God possesses every perfection in Himself. Creation was not *for* anything — it exhibits a "purposiveness without purpose", in Kant's words. Standing or kneeling before our Maker and Creator, the creature can only say *me voici*, in Levinas's sense.

God is depth and silence. He is the silent, Absolute abyss of nothingness as well as being the supreme Word. God is nothing. Such is the apophatic way. The Godhead has no name — He is the Unnameable and Ineffable One — the silent *desert*.

God gives birth to His son in the Ground of the soul. This is how Eckhart understood it. Try to see God in God — look out from within the very heart of God. For Aquinas, the world proves God; for Eckhart, God proves the world. Everything is not. The world is *not* God; its emptiness reflects Him. God even is not. *God is divine desire*. There is always paradox at the heart of Christianity.

A monk is someone who concentrates on the space between this world and the next and a monastery is the place he does it in. When I go to Glenstal I bring a part of the world with me to that enchanted, Catholic and pagan place but do I bring some monastic values back out into the world with me? You do not have to live in a monastery in order to be a monk. It's about attitude.

Religious life is rhythm, balance — and this too: a one-pointed energy and attention: the vertical irruption (and interruption) of the Other who is also the One.

When two or three are together, the shadow of God sometimes passes (*confere* Levinas). We abide in the shade and shelter of the Almighty.

To be a Christian is to live the resurrected life. Christianity? — being alive. Energetic. Attending. *Décreation à la* Simone Weil, which Iris Murdoch renders into "unselfing". The ego is fat and illusion-making.

Christianity is more than practice and being in belief. God's being is beyond being. God beyond God. I pray to God that He may rid me of God (Eckhart). "Deep calls unto deep", sings the Psalmist. Love seeks out the depths in things (Rilke).

Christ's aim? Total erasure. He sent us His spirit, who is the Source. The Persons of the Trinity are One. Our end, eschatologically: to enter into the very embrace of that Trinity. Hell is the refusal to enter. Hell is hubris. Hell: incarceration rather than incarnation.

Fear is not love's opposite. Nor is hate. Hate is a passion. Love is love's opposite.

The Kerygma: *Kenosis*. Mine and His.

Let me conclude with some short extracts which I wrote for *Stories of Faith* on a Jesuit website. My contribution was entitled "A Philosopher's Search for Meaning":

> I would describe myself as a seeker, searching for God within the Catholic Tradition. I believe in a God who is both transcendent and immanent. I believe in angels. Perhaps Aquinas's five arguments for the existence of God failed to prove His existence but they did succeed in showing that faith could be reasonable. . . . I find it hard to pray and practise my faith. I am unable to picture Heaven and conceive of everlasting happiness. . . . Sometimes, the thought of death (and living again) terrifies me. I wonder about my Judgement. I worry: do I really live according to the dictates of the Gospel and the law of love? Everywhere, I sense the Spirit at work. I feel the absent presence of my God in the world . . . as I lift my hands up to the holy place. I ponder on the Mystery and ask "why?" Life is marginally meaningful to me only in so far as it is prolonged in post-mortem existence. I pray on bended knee with a bowed head before Him who made me, sometimes in tears and sometimes smiling, mostly in agony.

Chapter 3

BEYOND BELIEF AND UNBELIEF: THE GOD QUESTION IN A TIME OF HOMELESSNESS

Hugh Cummins

I

My faith, if such it be called, is a great mystery to me. Though not without its consolations, I tend to think of it, after Augustine, as a special kind of "restlessness" rather than a reassuring possession. Restlessness is obviously not a very comfortable state. It even suggests possession in another sense, a sense in which one's autonomy and self assurance are *dis*possessed by the thought of something Other. To a certain extent, therefore, I would endorse the Augustinian gloss offered by the German theologian Jurgen Moltmann: ". . . faith, wherever it develops into hope, causes not rest but unrest, not patience but impatience. It does not calm the unquiet heart, but is itself this unquiet heart in man".[1] Alongside faith and hope, the third "theological virtue" is usually translated as love or charity. I prefer to speak of desire, a much explored theme both in psychoanalysis and in recent philosophy. To Moltmann's gloss, then, I would add that the restlessness born of faith and hope is related, via desire, to an Other. But this desire also involves a waiting on the Other, a *passionate* waiting that is, as the etymology of the word suggests, at the same time *patient*. Divine desire thus both seeks and waits, is at once active and receptive. It can abide patiently in its restlessness, like the Psalmist whose soul waits for the Lord even "more than those who watch for the morning" (Ps 130: 6-7).

Here I must qualify what is, perhaps, a somewhat premature declaration. What faith I can speak of arrived after many years of an atheism I do not expect to fully surpass. And yet there it was, unexpectedly, this frail shoot that had somehow pushed its way up through my Godless garden. How long had it been there? Who had planted the seed while my back was turned?

I experienced no dramatic conversion, no Vision Splendid, no divine summons or life-transforming event. In fact I continued — and continue — to experience what I long took to be the justification of my atheism — that is, to use a formulation of Sartre's, that "The absence of God was to be read everywhere".[2] What, then, had changed? I am not comfortable with the term "believer", which is why the question "Do you believe in God?" tends to reduce me to silence. For whether the response is positive or negative, question and answer alike, it seems to me, remain doomed to a certain reduction, a reduction to what Martin Buber would call an I–It relation. Nor is it a case of agnosticism, if this means some kind of detached neutrality in the absence of positive or negative "evidence". If agnosticism has a role to play, and it does, I like to think of it as a committed agnosticism, an agnostic faith. Beyond the temptations of belief or unbelief, then, I prefer to think of myself, to use a currently fashionable term, as a "person of faith".

What does it mean to speak of a faith that is beyond belief or unbelief? What relation, if any, might such a faith have to the determinate and specific *religions* of monotheism (Judaism, Christianity, Islam)? The second question bears on another theme that will surface frequently in the following — I mean the theme of home and homelessness. Homelessness is of course a pressing and ongoing social problem. But it is also, together with the quest for a home from which it is inseparable, one of the great themes of human existence. Religion, in its etymological sense of "binding-together" (*re-legere*), has in some ways functioned as an answer to this quest or (quest)ion. However, it has also in turn questioned the "solutions". As the Polish philosopher Leszek Kolakowski has put it:

> Throughout its history religion has told us that we are
> "elsewhere". This means that we have a home where we be-
> long. To be in exile is our permanent condition on earth.[3]

Philosophy too, from its beginnings, has expressed a primordial sense of displacement or homelessness. For the pre-
Socratic Empedocles, life is "a journey abroad", an idea that
extends through the Pythagoreans and Plato and echoes
throughout the philosophical tradition. In the twentieth century,
Martin Heidegger announced that "Homelessness is coming to
be the destiny of the world",[4] a destiny consequent upon our
inability to dwell in the truth of Being, and he quoted approv-
ingly a fragment of Novalis: "Philosophy is homesickness, an
urge to belong everywhere".[5] Finally, in this context, Martin
Buber has stated:

> In the history of the human spirit, I distinguish between ep-
> ochs of habitation and epochs of homelessness. In the for-
> mer, man lives in the world as in a house, as in a home; in
> the latter, man lives in the world as in an open field and at
> times does not have four pegs with which to set up a tent.[6]

In what follows I would like to make salient a certain tension between belief and unbelief and between home and homelessness.
Ultimately in each case the tension is not resolvable in terms of
one or the other. I will also be seeking to trace a movement in
which absence becomes transformed into something that remains absence and yet is not reducible to mere negation. This
movement will be filtered through a consideration of the three
thinkers on whom I have chosen to focus. The place of the first is
long established in my affections; the other two are of more recent acquaintance but no less important on what for me has become a faith journey. Finally, I wish to work through the
hypothesis that faith, in conjunction with hope and desire, transcends belief and unbelief even as it finds expression in both.

II

The Jewish experience lies at the heart of the three monotheistic faiths and of faith as such. This takes the form of a journey
into the unknown that is both a leavetaking and an orientation

towards a new possibility. Jewish thinkers, or rather thinkers whose Jewish background informs crucial aspects of their life and work, will figure exclusively below: Freud, Levinas and Derrida. Because the issues raised are also philosophical, however, the Greek experience is inescapable. Philosophy, as it arose among the ancient Greeks, emphasises knowledge rather than faith. But knowledge is also identified with love, as "love of wisdom" (*philo-sophia*). This love or *eros* is directed towards an origin rather than an end, or towards an end that is at the same time an origin. It seeks to recover an ultimate or pre-existing ground, beyond the contingencies of time and history, even though this recovery unfolds through dialogue and dialectic. Philosophy for the Greeks therefore tends to privilege being over becoming, knowing over doing, the eternal over the temporal. Truth emerges through access to an unchanging realm exemplified by the Platonic Forms rather than through the Divine-human encounter of the Hebrew experience in time. To put it crudely and simplistically: the Greek emphasis is metaphysical, the Hebrew existential.

The above distinctions are not absolute and even to posit them is inevitably falsifying. The Hebrew scriptures contain "wisdom literature" and the concerns of Greek philosophy have also been existential. The fact is that Hebrew and Greek currents merge inextricably in the history of western thought and beyond, especially in Christianity.

The Greek current will be represented here implicitly only, to the extent that it informs, even through opposition, the thought of the Jewish thinkers on whom I wish to focus.

* * *

The rudiments of Freud's critique of religion are well known. Religious beliefs have their origin in the childhood experiences of helplessness and dependency, and in the attendant need of a strong and loving protector, a role that for Freud is usually played by the father. Because the adult also experiences vulnerability and dependency, an even more exalted father-figure is required. The omnipotent God of the religions is thus the father of childhood writ large and projected skywards. The father-complex is such, however, that this figure will prove both friendly and unfriendly, acting as protector and judge, consoler and accuser. Religious systems, moreover, are worldviews (*weltanschauungen*) in which all the perplexities of human existence are given a coherent explanation, so that even death ceases to be a real threat. In short, religious beliefs and systems serve as "containers" for anxiety. They are "illusions" in the special sense that Freud gives to this term, a belief strongly motivated by or derived from a wish.[7]

Crucially for Freud, illusions are not necessarily false and their truth-content cannot be evaluated by psychoanalysis. He thus avoids what philosophers have called the "genetic fallacy", the idea that the truth-content of a belief or claim can be ascertained by examining its origins. Freud therefore does not seek to disprove the existence of God. As he put it, "We can only regret that certain experiences in life and observations in the world make it impossible for us to accept the premise of the existence of . . . a Supreme Being".[8] Finally, it remains an open question whether the God of the religions is a human projection, whatever the origins of this projection.

Freud once famously referred to himself as "a Godless Jew". His relationship with religion and the God question, however, is far too complex to be measured by a simple ascription of atheism. Indeed, as far as his famous self-description goes, the noun is every bit as worthy of reflection as the adjective. Freud's Jewishness is attested to not merely by his relentless iconoclasm but by his affirmation of what he called the "historical" as opposed to the "material" truth of monotheism. He also identified strongly with the primary Jewish iconoclast, Moses, and he once wrote to Lou Andreas Salomé that the figure of Moses had haunted him all his life. In 1914 he published a psychoanalytic study of Michelangelo's famous sculpture of Moses, and in the last five years of his life he worked on what was also to become the last book he published, *Moses and Monotheism*.

In developmental terms, monotheism, according to Freud, constituted a crucial advance for civilisation. The Jews were prohibited from making images of God and enjoined to worship an invisible God. God was no longer to be identified with the various phenomena of nature as in the polytheistic religions. This movement from a belief tied to a sense perception to a be-

lief founded on an inference and a hypothesis is analogous for
Freud to the transition from a matriarchal to a patriarchal culture. This amounted to a triumph of intellect over sensuality, or
in other words instinctual renunciation and sublimation. Hence
the unique intellectual contribution of the Jews to civilisation.
Moreover, from the time of the destruction of the temple in Jerusalem by Titus, "the Holy Writ and intellectual concern with it
were what held the scattered people together".[9]

The transition to monotheism and to patriarchal culture are
together in turn for Freud analogous to the role played by the
Oedipus complex in the development of the individual. In the
Oedipus complex, it is the intervention of the father that prohibits an incestuous union with the mother based on supply and
demand and on the immediate satisfaction of instinctual needs.
The French psychoanalyst Jacques Lacan will speak of the "pa-
ternal function", indicating that this intervention does not necessarily imply an empirically present father. In Lacan's
structural analysis, what is important is the introduction of a
third term into the mother–child relation. But for both Freud and
Lacan, intervention takes the form of a prohibition. Only thus
can a gap be created between demand and its object, and a
space of deferral opened that allows for sublimation and for future participation in society. This gap cannot but be experienced initially as an affliction, a wound: this is the symbolic
meaning of castration which, as Lacan will later theorise it, per-
tains to both men and women. The affliction or privation, however, is a blessing in disguise: it is what will enable the subject
to move from a register of need and demand to a register of desire. Analogously, monotheism prohibits a relation to the divine
based on the sensual, the visible, the immediate and the ma-
nipulable. At the same time it points to the invisible, the not-yet,
the journey, the promise of what is to come.

For Freud the historical truth of monotheism consists in the
identification with a single figure, Moses, an Egyptian murdered
by his early Semitic followers. The veneration of Moses by later
followers becomes the basis of a projection resulting in the idea
of a single God. From another perspective, however, what
emerges more tellingly from Freud's text is the simultaneous rupture and advance that he associates with monotheism. Pointing to

the overlapping and transitional nature of this development, as religious scholars have done, should not obscure its dramatic, and indeed traumatic, character. The Oedipus complex too is never fully surpassed. Ultimately Freud's analysis can be read as true to his Jewish heritage: monotheism is at once a form of "disenchantment", a de-divinising of the world of natural gods, and a "baptism of desire" for the God who is Wholly Other.

This disenchantment always runs the risk of an atheism that in the Jewish tradition is nevertheless preferable to idolatry. Atheism, as Emmanuel Levinas has implied, is in this sense "half-right". As one commentator on Levinas has stated:

> Idolatry means to think God in terms of the fears and expectations of human beings. [Levinas] thinks that the particular way of the Jewish sages consists precisely in breaking with this ancient conception of the sacred and in teaching how to seek God on the basis of a separation or even atheism.[10]

Freud's atheism is clearly a Jewish phenomenon in that it lives out this separation as a refusal of idols. It is precisely for this reason that the God question obsessed Freud to the end. But if he was thus "half-right" to the end, he was also fully Jewish in his intellectual concern with Holy Writ. To the philosophers who hoped to rescue the God of religion with an abstract principle, he recommended the warning words that are also the foundation of Jewish monotheism: "Thou shalt not take the name of the Lord thy God in vain!"[11]

III

For Levinas as for Freud, the God question involves both a leave-taking and a journey. Where Freud looks to Moses, the bearer of the law, the exemplary figure for Levinas is Abraham, the "father of faith". Levinas makes a sharp distinction between the Hebrew Abraham and the Greek Ulysses, the latter representing philosophy's quest for a return to some primordial foundation:

> To the myth of Ulysses returning to Ithaca we would like to oppose the story of Abraham leaving his country forever to go to a still unknown land and forbidding his servant to take even his son back to the point of departure.[12]

The wanderings of Ulysses have as their ultimate goal a home-coming, a return to what is already familiar. Abraham, in contrast, journeys into the unfamiliar, the unknown, the unseen, towards a home that is promised but that he will never fully inhabit. Abraham is a perpetual stranger, a nomad between two homes, yet it is from him that the Children of God, "as numberless as the stars", will descend.

The theme of a journey from the familiar into the unfamiliar is sounded at the outset of Levinas's major work, *Totality and Infinity*. He begins by quoting Rimbaud's celebrated dictum, "The true life is absent" (*La vraie vie est absente*), usually rendered in English as "Life is elsewhere". This sense of "restlessness", of an ever-present gap between desire and fulfilment, of an Other that always eludes our grasp and our understanding, is for Levinas the basis of metaphysics. Thus:

> Metaphysics . . . is turned toward the "elsewhere" and the "otherwise" and the "other". For in the most general form it has assumed in the history of thought it appears as a movement going forth from a world that is familiar to us . . . from an "at-home" . . . which we inhabit, toward an alien "outside-of-oneself" . . . toward a yonder.[13]

For Levinas, the history of philosophy has testified to this movement at privileged moments but has for the most part resisted it. In seeking to re-present what is Other and absent, philosophy has deployed concepts and categories that merely serve to reduce the Other to the Same. Here knowledge becomes, as Levinas says, "an adequation (an equating) between thought and what it thinks",[14] that is to say between thought and reality. But the Other cannot be reduced to knowledge; the Other cannot be known. Knowledge, ultimately, is an affair of the self (individual or communal), of its modes of representation and its norms of coherence. Striving to comprehend and assimilate what is Other, the self denies what is different and reduces the foreign to the familiar.

The Other, according to Levinas, is beyond representation, *in*adequate, exterior, infinitely exceeding all attempts at comprehension or "totalisation". This applies also to the other person, whether friend or stranger, loved one or enemy. How, in that case, are human relations and sociality possible? Here it is important to qualify what Levinas means by Other. The Other is not simply the empirical other before me but the Otherness of this other, that which lies outside my sphere of mastery or comprehension. The Other as such is always a stranger, even the loved one.

Sociality, as distinct from the functional anonymity of civic life, is made possible by an exposure to what Levinas calls the "face" of the Other. Importantly, the term "face" as Levinas uses it does not simply refer to the physiognomy of the other person. The face is the "trace" of the Other passing by me and beyond me yet also calling out to me. This call of the Other usurps self-possession with a question, a demand, a supplication. Ultimately, what is revealed in the face is the Other's nakedness and mortality. But if not reducible to physiognomy, the face at the same time retains a corporeal dimension. It inhabits, in effect, a borderline region between the visible and the invisible. Young or old, the ageing face of the Other is the remnant of someone who has already passed by. In the signs of its ageing, the face is "a trace of itself"; "it says *adieu, à-Dieu* — or simply farewell".[15]

Ethics also involves an exposure to the Other, an Other who is not reducible to knowledge or comprehension. Nevertheless, the Other calls for a response, which I am free to grant or withhold. It is not, it should be noted, a question of "empathy". Empathy, to the extent that it implies comprehension, is in fact a denial of the Other. Nor is it a question of "altruism" in any conventional or traditionally philosophical sense. For Levinas, the relation to the Other is asymmetrical and cannot be subsumed by any third term. Self and Other, in short, do not form a "set", even the set implied by the term "relationship".

What sustains the ethical relation to the Other is "desire", which Levinas, like Lacan, distinguishes sharply from need. Need presupposes a lack that can be filled or satisfied by an object, just as hunger is satisfied when food is assimilated and transformed into energy for the body. Desire, on the other hand, is incommensurate with any object and cannot be satisfied. As Levinas puts it, "Desire is like goodness — the Desired does not fulfil it but deepens it".[16]

It is through desire that I respond to the call of the Other, a call that comes, as it were, from "above", from the infinite or the "Most-High". The dimension of height does not open onto the heavens but onto the invisible, onto what is absent and yet revealed in the trace, in the "epiphany of the face". For Levinas, desire of the Other is thus receptive rather than seeking, not by way of symmetry or rapport but as an eruption of the "more" in the "less".

* * *

Exposure to the Other, the Stranger, is preceded for Levinas by a kind of "at-homeness". The ego, in its sensuality and enjoyment of the familiar, comes to be "at home with itself".[17] This home stands opposed to the oppressive indifference of Being, what Levinas calls the *il y a*, and within its protective space the ego becomes a "name in the anonymity of night".[18] The *il y a* is the mute thereness of a world that cares nothing for us. Levinas uses the French term in marked contrast to the German *es gibt* of Heidegger, the latter conveying the sheer gratuity and giftedness of Being. The *il y a* is other but not absolutely Other. It can be transformed by the ego through acts of labour and absorbed as material for the ego's needs. In this appropriation of the unfamiliar, the ego comes to be at home in the world.

At the centre of Levinas's thought is a journey away from the "at-home" so conceived, a journey that is at the same time the beginning of the ethical relation to the Other. This relation is made possible by a new kind of home or "ethos". This home between homes, as it were, is not a secure possession. Its chief characteristic, in fact, is that its security has been breached by the stranger who "paralyses possession". Again the figure of Abraham is exemplary for Levinas. Having left the secure and prosperous home of his ancestors, Abraham journeys in search of a new home promised by God and becomes a tent-dweller. What is significant for Levinas here is that Abraham leaves the flaps of his tent open to the stranger, and thus to the angel who turns out to be an incarnation of God.

* * *

Ethics, as Levinas has said, is "first philosophy", a term formerly applied to traditional metaphysics and the philosophy of
Being (ontology). But the absolutely Other, the Other of what
Levinas calls "metaphysical desire", cannot be identified with
anything that comes to presence in Being. Philosophy therefore
must resist "the urge to belong everywhere" as Heidegger, after Novalis, would have it. For to be at home everywhere
amounts to a colonising of the Other, a temptation that Heidegger notoriously failed to resist when he espoused the cause of
National Socialism in 1933. This, and his subsequent silence on
the holocaust, Levinas found difficult to forgive. What emerges
from the case of Heidegger and the Nazis is a stark reminder
that the search for home has its pathologies as well as its pa-
thos. But this is also true of the Jewish experience, a fact that
should not be obscured by uncritical philo-Semitism.

It is perhaps with this in mind that Levinas, who lost members of his own family in the holocaust, recommends "insomnia" as a perpetual watching over the Other. Insomnia is thus a
form of desire, desire for the absolutely Other. This desire is
what keeps love vigilant and resists appropriating the Other to
the Same. It also resists the mutual appropriation that becomes
the sleep of an *egoisme à deux*. Desire, in short, lifts love onto
an ethical level from which it would otherwise tend to fall back
into itself.

* * *

Levinas's philosophical preoccupations can all be seen to crys-
tallise around the question of God. This ultimate question is always approached indirectly, with endless qualifications and
caveats. Nowhere does Levinas speculate on the nature of God,
either in philosophical or theological language. The absolute
Otherness of God is irreducible to the Supreme Being, First
Mover or *Ens causa sui* of the philosophers, and also irreducible
to an object of faith or religious experience. Levinas's concern,
he has stated, is merely to describe the circumstances in which
the idea of God "comes to mind" from outside the self and its
constructions. The philosophical tradition, despite its predomi-
nantly totalising tendency, also provides examples of what can
strike thought from outside itself and remain irreducible to

Being, knowledge or experience. One such example is Descartes's "idea of the infinite" as he introduces it in the third meditation.

For Descartes the idea of the infinite is beyond anything that a finite creature could independently conceive. This suggests that the idea was implanted from outside the subject or the *cogito* and thus constitutes a proof of God's existence. It is God, finally, who underwrites the truth of those certainties established by the *cogito*, including the truth of its own existence. Levinas is not interested in proofs for God's existence but in Descartes's notion of "a relation with a being that maintains its total exteriority with respect to him who thinks it".[19] This notion, moreover, destabilises the celebrated autonomy of the Cartesian ego, revealing its purported identity to be in fact given by an Other.

The idea of the infinite does not for Levinas inhabit the mind as a presence, or as a concept that would re-present what is absent. Rather it evokes "metaphysical desire" as a movement towards what is endlessly beyond comprehension or possession. Levinas frequently uses the term *à-Dieu* (to-God) rather than *Dieu* (God) in order to convey the idea of an approach that continually falls short of encounter; at the same time the French word *adieu* is implied, indicating a farewell to the notions of presence and possession. Crucially, for Levinas, we approach the absolutely Other, or God, only through exposure to the Otherness of the neighbour, which is to say the Stranger.

In the epiphany of the "face" of the Other, God reveals himself as the divine absence that nevertheless leaves a "trace" as it passes, like a footprint in the sand. Central for Levinas here is the text of Exodus 33: 22-23, where God covers Moses with has hand to prevent him from seeing his face as he passes by. What Moses sees is the track or the trace of God's passing. Thus, according to Levinas, "To be created after God's image (*vestigi imago Dei*) does not mean that we are icons of God but that we are following in the track of his footprints".[20]

Levinas does not pose the God question in terms of belief or unbelief. The existence of God cannot be proved and is not fundamentally a question of belief or unbelief. For this reason, as he stated in his interview with Richard Kearney:

> I have tried to think of God in terms of desire, a desire that cannot be filled or satisfied — in the etymological sense of *satis*, measure . . . In this sense, our desire for God is without end or term: it is interminable, because God reveals himself as absence rather than presence. . . . Furthermore, when we say that God cannot satisfy man's desire, we must add that the insatisfaction is itself sublime. . . . In the infinite order, the absence of God is better than his presence; and the anguish of man's concern and searching for God is better than consummation or comfort.[21]

Such is what Levinas calls a "religion for adults", where God figures as a question rather than an answer and the search is more important than the solution. Thus Levinas proposes what at first appears to be a startling reversal: the privileging of time over eternity. Time is superior to eternity because "To be in eternity is to be *one*, to be oneself eternally", whereas "To be in time is to be for God (*être à Dieu*), a perpetual leavetaking (*adieu*)".[22] The apparent reversal is in fact consistent with the Hebrew view of history as the chosen site of the Divine–human encounter. Time is not a ripple on the lake of eternity (the Same) but the royal road to the not-yet, to the Other and to God (*à-Dieu*).

IV

Like the word "belief", the word "faith" scarcely figures in Levinas's vocabulary. He has said that the only faith to which he is willing to testify publicly is in the wisdom of the Talmudic sages. In the naming of the absolutely Other as God, however, there is at least an implicit faith or trust. His thought thus lies within broadly theistic parameters and inhabits a particular Jewish tradition of reflection and interpretation.

For Jacques Derrida, whose work has come to owe an increasing debt to Levinas, the boundaries between theism and atheism have all but collapsed. Derrida is widely known as the father of "deconstruction" but in recent years he has become preoccupied with religious themes in a way that has surprised both disciples and detractors. Of his own position on the God question he has said, "I quite rightly pass for an atheist".[23] However, there is an ambiguity in this statement that becomes even more pronounced when considered alongside a possibility to which Derrida also adverts — that "the extreme and most consequent form of declared atheism will always have testified to the most intense desire of God".[24] Clearly a special kind of atheism is involved here, and for Derrida it is linked to the notions of desire and the Other. Richard Kearney offers this gloss on Derrida's position:

> Atheism is less a refusal of God . . . for Derrida, than a renunciation of a specific God (or Gods) — a renunciation which could almost be said to serve as condition of possibility of a God still to come, still to be named.[25]

Derrida welcomes the advent of the Other as a possibility that might transform our ways of thinking and doing — in relation to philosophy, politics and ethics, for example, but also in relation to the religious themes he has recently explored: the gift, hospitality, testimony and forgiveness. And yet: is Derrida not famously, infamously even, associated with the expression: "There is nothing outside the text"? Importantly for Derrida, "text" does not only refer to words on a page. A text is something "woven", as in "textile", and for Derrida extends to the various historical, social, cultural and political networks in which we are embedded, if not quite at home. The text is *The Matrix*, to invoke the 1999 movie and its recent sequels. It can be interpreted and "read" from within but we cannot hack our way out of it. To say there is nothing outside the text, or context, is to say that there is no outside reference point, no ahistorical "view from nowhere" from which the meaning of any text can be determined.

The Other of the text is in a sense the absence of this reference point or ultimate origin, a void as it were around which the text is constructed but whose effect or "trace" continually threatens to destabilise such constructions, or rather to reveal their *inherent* instability, which is to reveal them *as* constructions. Deconstruction therefore is not destruction; it is an attempt to accede to new possibilities, new forms of discourse that yet acknowledge the Other around which all discourse is constructed.

In this desire and welcoming of the Other, to which deconstruction testifies, Derrida sees the repetition of a traditional religious structure that he names the "messianic". At the same time, he refuses to align himself with the content of the specific religions that he refers to, with the monotheistic religions in mind, as the "messianisms". The latter, for Derrida, tend towards ideological closure because the Other to whom they are pledged is at the same time excluded by specific thematisations and representations. These merely serve to pull the Other back into the circle of the same, condemning the messianisms to mutual hostility and war.

Unlike Levinas, Derrida will not name the absolutely Other as "God". As he puts it, "Every other is absolutely Other",[26] whether man, woman, God or animal. Derrida is not arguing here for inclusiveness but for an inescapable "undecidability". There is no certain knowledge whether the Other of desire, Levinas's footprint in the sand, is a stranger, God or monster — to invoke the three "undecidables" of Richard Kearney's recent book.[27] For Derrida, the advent of the Other is not always the Good News. The stranger in my house may wish to burn it down; the God who comes always when I least suspect, "like a thief in the night" (1 Thess. 5:2), may turn out to be indeed a thief, or some demonic projection or hallucination of my own. It is for this reason, the undecidability of the absolutely Other, that faith figures more prominently in Derrida's lexicon than that of Levinas.

Faith for Derrida is inseparable from desire and trust, but also from "fear and trembling". It is only thus that the desire of God survives the atheism that Derrida professes. Moreover, the distinction that he posits between a messianic structure and the content of the messianisms is not absolute; Derrida has himself drawn on the deconstructive potential to be found in Judaeo-Christianity, in "restless" texts that endlessly put themselves in question and open themselves to re-interpretation. For all that, the God of desire, the other name of desire in faith and hope, is a strictly futural God, a God that even the word "God" merely gestures towards, a God that has yet to be invented (*in-venir*). Such is what Derrida calls a "religion without religion", a "desire beyond desire" that continually suspends its own momentum in order to keep itself alive.

V

Freud, Levinas and Derrida all demonstrate a relation to the God question that is uniquely Jewish in its restless anti-idolatry. Among them, only Levinas emerges from the attendant "risk of atheism" as avowedly theist. But the absent God to whom Levinas testifies seems so drained of content that at least one commentator has wondered how his position can be distinguished from atheism.[28] For Levinas, however, as for Martin Buber who Levinas has acknowledged as a precursor despite crucial differences, the question of God is inseparable from the sphere of the interhuman. The meaning of God's absence is, in a sense, precisely this deflection onto the human Other who yet, as absolutely Other, speaks from "above". Thus:

> It is not by superlatives that we can think of God but by trying to identify the particular interhuman events that open towards transcendence and reveal the traces where God has passed.[29]

Levinas, finally, has sought to bring a new sobriety to the God question. He rejects all forms of religious "enthusiasm" that would speak of possession by the godhead or of mystical fusion. And yet what has been described as a "hyperethics", in which the self is always "hostage" to the Other, clearly points to another kind of excess. The possibility of manipulation or even abuse by the Other is never properly addressed. Moreover, in his recommendation of "insomnia" as a perpetual watching over the Other, the question arises: can insomnia itself become intoxicating, indeed toxic? Such questions continue to be debated by Levinas scholars. What cannot be doubted, however, is Levinas's achievement in returning the God question to a central position in contemporary philosophy.

Derrida, on the other hand, "passes for an atheist", with all the ambiguities that this formulation suggests. He has also meditated on the problematics of "the divine name" in a way that reflects his Jewish background. In the Hebrew tradition, it is possible to recognise and relate to the revealed God only on the basis of a name; but a too confident naming implies possession and risks the purely imaginary familiarity that leads to idolatry. It is this ambivalence that led pious Jews to impose a taboo on pronouncing the "name" revealed to Moses, *Yahweh*, and to retain the consonantal form, the "tetragrammaton" YHWH, even after vowels were added to the Hebrew scriptures in the middle ages.

The name that God revealed to Moses (*Yahweh*: "I am who am"/"I am who shall be") is a name only in a qualified sense. It could be read in fact as the withholding of a name, so that the spoken words become, in a sense, the substitute for name. This substitute is in turn inherently unstable, and undergoes a series of further displacements to become the God of Abraham, Isaac, Jacob etc. Thus begins the long history of displacement through the various Hebrew names for God. All are marked by the absence, the trace of the unknown name in which full presence is to be manifested.

According to Derrida, our names for God, including "God" presumably, are like arrows which if they were ever to reach their target would only wound it.[30] We "save the name" (*Sauf le nom*), respect the secret of the name, through substitution and displacement. Thus Derrida precedes his declaration of "atheism" with another declaration: "The constancy of God in my life goes by other names."[31] Among these other names, it can be assumed from his later work, are to be included justice, testimony, hospitality and forgiveness.

In comparison with Derrida's, Freud's atheism would appear to be unequivocal, whether "half-right" or not. His Other, moreover, is the unconscious rather than the absolutely Other of Levinas. But the unconscious too, at least as Lacan formulates it, is absolutely Other, is "the discourse of the Other". I am not master in my own house, as Freud said of the ego. In Freud's willingness to explore the God question to the end, it is possible to discern the trace of this Other discourse. Faith at its purest and truest may have as its precondition that it forget itself, translating itself into the assumed burden and orientation of a life. Conversely, articulations of belief and unbelief at the level of the ego may be so much hot air. I venture this as a possibility only, though I suspect that it is more than half-true. I also acknowledge a long tradition stemming from St Anselm and St Augustine that speaks of "faith in search of understanding".

Moreover, articulation as a new way of speaking, "the talking cure", is one of the goals of psychoanalysis. In relation to Freud, however, I hold with the above. "Let your left hand not know what your right hand is doing" are the words attributed to Jesus. But it is perhaps one of Dostoyevsky's characters who offers the best clue to the truth of Freud's desire: "The absolute atheist stands on the last rung but one before most absolute faith."[32]

For the "absolute atheist", the God question remains a question, an Other that is not reducible to the Same of science. Freud's atheism, despite his scientific language and his need for scientific credibility, is thus to be distinguished from that of a scientist like Richard Dawkins. Psychoanalysis falls short of scientific credibility to the extent that it remains haunted and destabilised by its Other, without which it becomes yet one more form of idolatry.

VI

The God question has returned to contemporary philosophy in what many regard as a "post-religious" age. This implies a new kind of homelessness, an "unbinding" of traditional practices and beliefs that once provided a locus of belonging and a framework for making sense of the fundamental questions of life and death. Others have been inclined to celebrate this development, as well as the loosening of other social structures like the nuclear family, welcoming a new freedom of choice and exploration. There are also signs, in Ireland as elsewhere, that this freedom can serve an increased rather than a diminished interest in religious questions. Usually this has been expressed in terms of "spirituality", whose advocates are often keen to distance themselves from religion and its burden of history and scandal. But whatever the nature of privatised spirituality or religion, it is no longer cognate with *religion* in its etymological sense of "binding-together".

In a sense, a faith that considers itself to be "beyond belief and unbelief" is also symptomatic of this new kind of homelessness. I do not, however, think a solution is to be found in spirituality alone, whether it be "new age" or "mind/body/spirit" or even the more searching and challenging forms that no doubt exist. Martin Buber has said that "even the sublimest spirituality is an illusion if not bound to the situation".[33] This is also true of faith, whose sphere is what Buber calls the "lived-concrete". But it is not faith but rather a kind of salvic knowledge or *gnosis* that much contemporary spirituality seeks. This is an instrumental knowledge through which magical forms of self-transformation can be effected, involving heightened forms of awareness and interconnection. Thus the individual liberated from older social bonds seeks to overcome what has proved to be an oppressive isolation.

On the other hand, it is clearly the case that the organised communal structures of religion have become increasingly "unhomely". Yet what is usually referred to as "the crisis of faith" can plausibly be regarded as an incipient feature of the time of unquestioned consensus. "Things fall apart", not haphazardly or in "mere anarchy" as Yeats has it, but along lines of tension that are present in the original construction.

The German philosopher Eric Voegelin once suggested that the cultural hegemony of Christianity was precisely what endangered Christian faith. In its worldly success and security, faith became infected with the illusions of *gnosis* or privileged knowledge that had accompanied Christianity as a temptation from the beginning. Thus faith became not what St Paul called it, "the substance of things hoped for", but rather the substance of things achieved. It was inevitable that such a phantasy would come to grief. One commentator has pointed to the possibly gnostic, or "crypto-gnostic" character of much Christian apologetics,[34] and Kierkegaard's distinction between "Christendom" and "Christianity" also comes to mind. For Voegelin, in contrast to this worldly self-assurance:

> Uncertainty is the very essence of Christianity. The feeling of security in "a world full of gods" is lost with the gods themselves; when the world is de-divinised, communication with the world-transcendent God is reduced to the tenuous bond of faith. . . . The bond is tenuous, indeed, and it may snap easily. The life of the soul in openness toward God, the waiting, the periods of aridity and dullness, guilt and despondency, contrition and repentance, forsakenness and hope against hope, the silent stirrings of love and grace,

> trembling on the verge of a certainty that if gained is loss —
> the very lightness of this fabric may prove too heavy a bur-
> den for men who lust for massively possessive experience.[35]

Voegelin provides a much needed reminder that the "lust for
massively possessive experience" is not restricted to the alternative spiritualities that have emerged in recent years. It has
always, to a greater or lesser extent, been a feature of established Christianity. When the "tenuous bond of faith" snaps the
result is not cognitive degree zero, nor those periods of anguish
that faith must necessarily live through, but a massive inflation
of the soul which is at the same time a form of closure.

* * *

"Religion for me has always been the wound, not the bandage."[36] The English television playwright Dennis Potter repeated what for him had become a favourite maxim in the
famous interview with Melvyn Bragg, broadcast shortly before
Potter's death in 1994. I was intrigued by this remark, for it was
clear that Potter was not simply condemning religion as the
cause of war or other ills. It is, of course, the antithesis of Marx's
"opium of the people" thesis. The following is an attempt to
elaborate on its possible meaning.

Religion is a form of discourse, that is, "a saying something
about something to someone". As such it is part of the social
bond and a private religion is as impossible as a private language. But the "about" of which religion speaks is especially
elusive. Derrida, it will be recalled, has pointed to an absence,
an Other that haunts all discourse. The word is not the thing;
there is no reference without difference. Religious discourse
too is organised around its Other, around something ineffable
that always threatens to destabilise its cultural expressions,
sometimes to the point of collapse, after which new or modified
expressions become necessary, new chains of discourse
around what is ultimately beyond symbolisation. The Other of
religion is thus not unlike the "navel" of the dream as Freud describes it, an unplumbable centre that remains resistant to all
interpretation. It is around this centre that is not a centre, whose
effect is precisely to *de*-centre — it is around this Other or

"thing" or wound that religion weaves what Lacan has called its "fabulous resources".

Religion, then, is a kind of binding that is also bound to its own unravelling, as is the earth that shall "grow old like a robe" (Is. 24:18-20) Religion is therefore wound *and* bandage, existing on the edge of things, in a borderline region between the speakable and the unspeakable. On this border we also encounter what Karl Jaspers has called "limit-situations", where suffering or death or evil confound all our attempts at comprehension and reveal to us our radical finitude. The ultimate limit-situation, perhaps, is human mortality and its spectre of final insignificance. "Shall we and all our lovely words vanish without a trace?" Shall we all have been speaking forgotten languages?" asks John Caputo in his book *On Religion*.[37] For Caputo, religion is also bound to *this* possibility, and is thus "co-constituted by the tragic sense, which is both the very sense that would undo it and the sense against which it itself takes shape".[38] But this "tragic sense of life", also explored by Unamuno, can become a form of *jouissance* or enjoyment, a masochistic indulgence which also tries to kill the Other, the Other that desire acknowledges as the unknown. Thus as Caputo also acknowledges: "For the religious sense of life the bonds of the present are not nailed down by necessity but broken open by the possible, by the possibility of the impossible".[39]

When Lacan spoke of religion's "fabulous resources" he was suggesting that such resources may be too fabulous, merely blinding us to the Other around which they are woven. Derrida's distinction between the messianic and the messianisms is an attempt to counter this tendency to exclude the Other. Faith, however, does not exist in a vacuum, and the God question is always in part an inherited question, mediated by previous explorations and interpretations. Faith can be centrifugal and centripetal, moving back and forth between the desert of the messianic, where it aligns itself with desire of the absolutely Other, and the shelter of the messianisms, where this desire is sustained by the hospitality of the specific religions. It is Caputo who recommends this to-and-fro movement. Here the religions, or the "determinate faiths", can be counted among those "groups of ideas" that the English poet and philosopher

T.E. Hulme called "huts for men to live in".[40] But again as Caputo reminds us, "the safety of these shelters is haunted by the unsettling thought of the searing desert sun and the numbing desert nights that lie outside their sheltering circles".[41]

* * *

Although denominationally restless, I acknowledge the text about Jesus as my immediate "horizon of waiting". Otherwise, I would speak of a "faith-context" rather than a "faith-content". "I have no idea what Christ actually said or did",[42] an Irish Benedictine monk said in a recent interview with the editor of this volume. I am happy to align myself with this confession! The four evangelists were "interpreters", subject like all of us to selection, omission, hyperbole, phantasy — as well as to the social, linguistic and artistic conventions of their local cultures. The figure of the historical Jesus moves through the Gospel texts as a trace, a footprint, an absence that yet haunts them. It is from this Other of the text, whose effect can be felt within the text, that extends, mediated by centuries of subsequent interpretation, the invitation to personal transformation and the promise of the Kingdom.

The resurrection of Jesus, as I understand it, belongs essentially to the future rather than the past. In other words it is not an achieved event but an ongoing possibility whose full realisation depends on our willingness to embody it and carry it forward in our own lives. Jesus' new body is the historical body of the community of the living and the dead, and as such it is only partly resurrected. This interpretation owes much to Hegel, with a crucial difference however: the promise is not a guarantee, nothing is predetermined.

In short, I am not certain about the "happy ending". After the cry of forsakenness, the God to whom Jesus offers up his spirit remains a silent and absent God. To dwell expectantly within the limits marked out by this silence and absence, and at the same time to offer up one's spirit, is for me the meaning of faith.

Who planted the seed while my back was turned? "God's a rumour", Dennis Potter said in the interview mentioned above. His absence, to recall Sartre, "[is] to be read everywhere". I have learned, I suppose, to listen to this rumour more attentively, and to read in this absence the trace of the absolutely Other. In faith I am happy to address this Other as God, but I am also mindful of the need to "save the name", the as yet unknown name.

In the meantime, the "between-time", I try to identify, to recall Levinas, "the particular interhuman events which open towards transcendence and reveal the traces where God has passed". I think of tender mercies, epiphanies of kindness and giftedness, as well as moments of obscure summons. Among the most precious gifts have been the words of others (shall they vanish without a trace?), to which a glance through the above will testify. But of course I mean words spoken as well, human words in which something of the Word came to pass, uttered by some who have also, as we say, passed on, *adieu, à-Dieu*.

"In the beginning was the Word" (John 1:1). But the word is already the mark or trace of God's passage into silence. It is what we are left with. As such it is always a human, or interhuman word. Through it, the text comes into being as a kind of home, something "woven-together". And yet to inhabit it too possessively is to fall into fundamentalism, to identify word and thing and thus exclude the Other.

I must acknowledge as a broader context, or further horizon, the text about Abraham. This "sojourner and stranger on the earth", in September 2002, made it to the cover of *Time* magazine. Post-11 September 2001, the featured article explored whether Abraham could be invoked as a peacemaker among the three religions that acknowledge him as their father.[43] Several months later his name was mentioned in news programmes, when the land from which he had set out was the scene of war between the representatives of two monotheistic cultures. This was also a war of words, a war between "keepers of the Book".

In his essay "Our Homeland, the Text", George Steiner recalls, as did Freud, how concern with a text had held the scattered Hebrew people together across long distances of space and time. What happened later, when the text became immobilised in a particular architectural space, leads Steiner to speculate that "Locked materially in a material homeland, the text may, in fact, lose its life force, and its truth value may be betrayed".[44] If we become "nomads of the word", however, the text itself becomes the homeland. As Steiner puts it, and we can substitute whatever architectural or institutional space comes to mind: "The Temple may be destroyed: the texts which it housed sing in the winds that scatter them."[45]

Notes

[1] Jurgen Moltmann, *Theology of Hope*, trans. James W. Leitch (London: SCM Press, 2002) 7.

[2] Simone de Beauvoir, *Adieu: A Farewell to Sartre*, trans. Patrick O'Brian (Penguin, 1985) 435.

[3] Leszek Kolakowski, *Metaphysical Horror* (Penguin, 2001), 30.

[4] Martin Heidegger, "Letter on Humanism", in *Basic Writings*, ed. David Farrell Krell (London: Routledge, 1993), 243.

[5] See Michael Zimmerman, *Heidegger's Confrontation with Modernity: Technology, Politics, Art* (Indiana University Press, 1990), 23.

[6] Martin Buber, "What is Man?", in *Between Man and Man*, trans. Robert Gregor Smith (Fontana, 1974), 157.

[7] See Sigmund Freud, "The Future of an Illusion" (Chapter VI), in *Civilisation, Society, Religion*, trans. James Strachey (Penguin Freud Library, Vol. 12, 1991).

[8] Sigmund Freud, "Moses and Monotheism", in *The Origins of Religion*, trans. James Strachey (Penguin Freud Library, Vol. 13, 1990), 370.

[9] Ibid., 362.

[10] See Catherine Chalier, "Levinas and the Talmud", in *The Cambridge Companion to Levinas*, ed. Simon Critchley and Robert Bernasconi (Cambridge University Press, 2002) 104-105.

[11] Sigmund Freud, *Civilization and its Discontents* (PFL, Vol. 12), 261.

[12] Quoted in Colin Davis, *Levinas: An Introduction* (Polity Press, 1996), 33.

[13] Emmanuel Levinas, *Totality and Infinity: An Essay on Exteriority*, trans. Alphonso Lingus (Pittsburgh: Duquesne University Press, 1969), 33.

[14] Emmanuel Levinas, *Ethics and Infinity: Conversations with Philippe Nemo, trans.* Richard A. Cohen (Pittsburgh: Duquesne University Press, 1982), 60.

[15] Bernard Waldenfels, "Levinas and the Face of the Other", in *Cambridge Companion to Levinas*, 77.

[16] Emmanuel Levinas, *Totality and Infinity*, 34.

[17] Ibid., 143.

[18] Quoted in Philip Blond, "Emmanuel Levinas: God and Phenomenology", in *Post-Secular Philosophy: Between Philosophy and Theology*, ed. Philip Blond (London, New York: Routledge, 1988), 211.

[19] Emmanuel Levinas, *Totality and Infinity*, 50.

[20] Quoted in Veronica Brady, "Postmodernism and the Spiritual Life", in *The Way: Review of Contemporary Christian Spirituality* (Vol. 36, No. 3, July 1996), 184.

[21] Richard Kearney, *Dialogues with Contemporary Continental Thinkers* (Manchester University Press, 1986), 68.

[22] Ibid., 59.

[23] Geoffrey Bennington and Jacques Derrida, "Circumfession", in *Jacques Derrida*, trans. G. Bennington (Chicago: University of Chicago Press, 1993), 155.

[24] Jacques Derrida, *On the Name*, ed. Thomas Dutoit, trans. David Wood, John P. Leavy, Jr., and Ian Mcleod (California: Stanford University Press, 1995), 36.

[25] Richard Kearney, *The God Who May Be: A Hermeneutics of Religion* (Indiana University Press, 2001), 71. My own exploration here of the thought of Levinas and Derrida, especially the latter, owes much to Kearney's treatment in Chapter Four of this book: "Desiring God".

[26] See ibid., 73-74, and Jacques Derrida, *On the Name*, 74.

[27] Richard Kearney, *Strangers, Gods and Monsters* (London, New York: Routledge, 2003). Importantly, Kearney does not finally accept the notion of radical "undecidability" and argues for a hermeneutics based on vigilance and discernment that can help to distinguish the malign from the benign Other.

[28] See Hillary Putnam, "Levinas and Judaism", in *Cambridge Companion to Levinas*, 53.

[29] Richard Kearney, *Dialogues with Contemporary Continental Thinkers*, 67.

[30] See Jacques Derrida, *On the Name*, 62–63.

[31] Bennington and Derrida, "Circumfession", in *Jacques Derrida*, 155.

[32] Dostoyevsky, *The Devils*, trans. David Magarshack (Penguin Classics, 1953/1971), 679.

[33] Quoted in Maurice Friedman, *Martin Buber's Life and Work: The Later Years, 1945–1965* (Wayne State University Press, 1988), 151.

[34] See Martin Henry, *On Not Understanding God* (Columba Press, 1997), 50. Henry sees in this tendency, which could also be described as "rationalist", a fear of the scepticism and doubt that have classically been regarded as the "arch-enemies" of Christianity. However, he points to another possibility that "defenders of the faith" might note with interest: ". . . could not scepticism itself, even an exasperated scepticism be interpreted as a philosophical echo of Christianity's belief in the transcendence of God? This belief relativises all merely worldly powers and human ambitions, but it only relativises them, it does not destroy or seek to destroy them. Thus it could be argued that the philosophical expression of its message with which Christianity could in present conditions be most comfortable is, precisely, scepticism." Ibid., 50.

[35] Eric Voegelin, *The New Science of Politics: An Introduction* (University of Chicago Press, 1952/1987), 122.

[36] From television interview with Melvyn Bragg, excerpted in *New Left Review* (No. 205, May/June, 1994), 132–3.

[37] John D. Caputo, *On Religion* (London, New York: Routledge, 2001), 119.

[38] Ibid., 120.

[39] Ibid., 123.

[40] T.E. Hulme, "Cinders", in *T.E. Hulme: Selected Writings*, ed. Patrick McGuinness (UK: Carcanet Press/Fyfield Books, 1998), 23.

[41] John D. Caputo, *On Religion*, 36.

[42] Stephen J. Costello, ed., *The Irish Soul: In Dialogue* (Dublin: The Liffey Press, 2001). See interview with Mark Patrick Hederman, 135.

[43] *Time*, 30 September 2002. See feature article by David Van Biema. One source mentioned in the article is the recently published *Abraham: A Journey to the Heart of Three Faiths* by Bruce Feiler.

[44] George Steiner, "Our Homeland, the Text", in *No Passion Spent: Essays 1978-1996* (London, Boston: Faber and Faber, 1996), 327.

[45] Ibid., 323.

Chapter 4

PLATO, PSYCHOANALYSIS AND RELIGION

Mitch Elliot

PHILOSOPHICAL BASES OF PSYCHOANALYSIS

Psychoanalysis was launched in the 1890s by Sigmund Freud, whose background was in medical research. Although an impressive amount of Freud's early work remains valid, it is also true to say that the body of psychoanalytic findings has expanded a great deal since the Freudian heyday of the 1920s. More significantly, psychoanalysis has grown well beyond the medico-scientific cause-and-effect outlook which was the cradle of its early days.

It is certainly true that our philosophical lenses influence what we see and what we miss; the selection of fish caught by a fisherman is influenced by the size of the holes in his net, and the strength of the string. On a second level, our philosophical standpoint will heavily affect how we assemble the raw data into metapsychological theory. Ptolemaic astronomy enabled accurate predictions to be made of the positions of the planets in the heavens — even though it represented them as being embedded in crystal spheres turning around the earth. It was still unthinkable that Earth, and her population of humans, might *not* be the centre of the universe. Thirdly, of course, one's philosophical spectacles influence what happens between analyst and patient in the consulting room.

Mainstream psychoanalysis in Europe has in the main sensibly adopted an existential view. I, the analyst, have my own baggage which I can only ever partly know. I will remain as open as possible to the utterances, the physical posture, the manoeuvrings of my patient. This particular one-to-one encounter will produce insights and understandings which will hopefully be useful and therapeutic. My experience is that this hope has been largely borne out, particularly if I am carefully selective of whom I take on as a patient.

This widely adopted existential clinical posture has been often supplemented by a mythological outlook. In human society, we are in groups influenced by a concatenation of cultural myths, which affect us mainly unconsciously. Analysis of the presence and effects of cultural or tribal myths in each individual was regarded as vital even in Freud's time, even in Freud's core group — Otto Rank's work on the *Myth of the Birth of the Hero*, for example, remains an important work. So the mythological viewpoint — including Lacan's interesting concept of the individual's personal mythology — cannot really be said to have been introduced to replace or offset Freud's medico-scientific bias: the mythic dimension was already there. The Jungian branch of the movement insisted (probably reasonably) on the presence of hereditary myths, and avoided (probably unreasonably) the biological factors almost completely for some decades.

Postmodern existentialism, however, has its pitfalls. It is not unreasonable to view the dominant thought-patterns, the major philosophical branches, of a culture, as in itself kind of mythology, characteristic of that culture in that time. Viewed in this way, postmodern existentialism could be seen as one reaction in the intellectual wing of our culture to the vicissitudes of the broader European culture — including the US and Australia — over the last century or two.

The popular fascination with the sinking of the *Titanic*, a true story of the twentieth century which has attained mythic status, cannot be explained by the magnitude of the disaster: far greater numbers were involved in other disasters. No: the *Titanic* fascinates us because we see this multi-layered, multi-class, splendid ship, called unsinkable, sailing into the sunset to its certain doom. And in us is a resonance with the doom of the proud, arrogant, multi-layered civilisation which produced the *Titanic*. This wider doom was to take a powerful lurch towards completion, like the lurch of the stricken liner, in the years immediately following the Titanic disaster, in the Great War of 1914–1918. By 1918, the three great feudal houses which had not been tamed by parliamentary democracy, now fell: the Romanovs of Russia, the Hohenzollerns of Prussia, and the Habsburgs of Austria. A system which had dominated Europe for twelve hundred years now lay in ruins. The abortive attempts to restore in fascism a kind of neo-feudal authority were in turn doomed: Hitler, Mussolini, Franco, and Salazar have all been swept from the stage. Even Lenin and Stalin may fit into this framework.

Hans Jonas, in his book *The Gnostic Religion*, was right to compare Gnostic pessimism with postmodern existentialism. Both philosophical stances were a reaction to the disappearance into a colder, wider world order, of a comfortable political landscape which had lasted for hundreds of years, and which previously had seemed eternal. But that period, like this, was an Interregnum; and postmodern existentialism, like Gnosticism, will be superseded by new cultural day-dreams.

Meanwhile, the clinical application of postmodern existentialism, has its dangers. As postmodernism is characterised by universal deconstruction, the postmodern analyst must be careful that over-zealous analysis may actually preclude the emergence of new intermediate structures in the client's psyche. Midwifing emergent structures is part of our task, it seems to me, as synthesis succeeds analysis. Some emergent structures will include what Winnicott might describe as "necessary illusions", and these must be respected for a time. Just as a baby dreams it is still in the womb when it is not. Just as variations of tooth-fairy religion seem to be a necessary precursor to deeper philosophical, or indeed theological views. And just as a patient's unreasonable, but useful, positive transference to the analyst is left unanalysed until the proper moment.

Early psychoanalysis in Ireland, of course, also went into the broader existential view — not limiting perception of what is called "significant" to the biologically based phenomena studied by Freud — and not excluding these phenomena either. And in Ireland the mythic dimension continued to be respected.

But the metapsychological constructions put together by early analysts in Ireland also came under the influence of what may be called the Platonic outlook.

FREUD AND THE AGE OF REASON

The Age of Reason is typified by the work of scientists, from Copernicus, Galileo, and Kepler, through Newton, to such nineteenth-century giants as Pasteur, Galvano and Rutherford. The work of René Descartes completed that of Newton, so that Newton's calculus could be graphically depicted using Cartesian co-ordinates. And it all seemed to work; there seemed to be a wonderful equivalence between mathematical models in the minds of men, and the actual workings of the visible and measurable external reality.

Two key concepts seem to characterise the Age of Reason. One is the assumption of verifiable cause-and-effect. Each action in the universe is the result of a prior cause; each action has knock-on results. Proceeding from this notion, which has been summarised as "the clockwork universe", we have the idea of deism. Where is God in all this? God, if one retained a belief in him at all — and many didn't — is the ultimate cause: the winder of the clock. The beauty of the stately wheeling of the planets is a divine beauty, the sign of the hand of the creator. But after setting it all in motion, the divine horologist left it all to tick away according to the divine laws and logic of the universal clockwork.

Freud, although he often showed that his actual views in practice could be broader, nevertheless remained heavily under the influence of the ethos in which he was reared. An early Freudian model of the human personality, the bipartite arrangement of ego and id, was based on the amoeba. At the core of the amoeba was its nucleus, with the genetic material — this corresponded to the id. Surrounding this core, and mediating with the environment, like the amoeba's membrane, was the ego. The fact that it took thirty years for Freud to separate out the superego as a distinct, crucial, mental agency, was possibly due to his reluctance to abandon the amoeba-like model.

Freud noted that in the individual's development, phases were traversed which replicated phases of development of humankind. This is again a medical concept, rooted in the observed fact that a human embryo goes through phases in which it seems identical to our evolutionary forebears; first fish-like, then mammalian, finally human. All this in amniotic fluid possessing the same salinity as the ancient seas where life originated. Freud borrowed a medical phrase and applied it to psychology: "ontogeny recapitulates phylogeny" — the individual development recapitulates ancestral/evolutionary development.

Thirdly, Freud saw personal decision as being produced by the balancing and unbalancing of forces. If a libidinal wish was stronger, it would prevail; if a countervailing prohibition was greater, then this would win out.

In *The Future of an Illusion* Freud took a formal position against the organised religions, particularly Christianity, as being a sort of societal neurotic phenomenon. He saw devotion to science, almost like a new religion, as the hopeful successor to organised religions. This view, of course, enthrones science at the expense of the neurotic organised religions. We note in passing that in this matter, as in many others, Freud's practice diverged from, and seems broader than, his theory. For describing the beneficial effects of psychoanalysis, Freud quoted the French doctor Ambroise Paré: *"je panse le plaie, mais Dieu la guérit"* (I dress the wounds, but God does the healing). I expect he saw "God" as a self-healing impetus in us all, which could become neurotically blocked; the action of psychoanalysis in healing was to remove these blocks to our natural self-healing, seen then perhaps as divine.

Under the impact of the twentieth-century scientific and philosophic advances, the clockwork universe of the Age of Reason faltered. Einstein's work showed a relativity of measurement depending on where you were and how fast you were moving. Heisenberg demonstrated the uncertainty of our knowing both position and velocity of subatomic particles, with the unsettling suggestion that maybe it wasn't just our *knowledge* that was uncertain, but perhaps the *actual quantities out there did not possess an independent value*. More recent work in what is called chaos mathematics seems to indicate a fundamental instability in a large number of phenomena which previously were considered very stable and potentially perfectly predictable. Perhaps orderly clusters or systems are in fact in the minority? And in Ireland Hanaghan was asking a disturbing question; in effect:

> If a psychoanalytic interpretation is the lock-step inevitable result of ironclad chains of cause-and-effect, if it was potentially predictable and inevitable twenty thousand years ago, is it true? Or is it merely another tick of the clockwork universe? What then is the "truth"?

In this environment of a renewed scientific humility — perhaps as profound as the Copernican revolution a few centuries earlier — psychoanalysis seemed to split in two main directions. The medicalised version of psychoanalytic therapy seemed for many to retreat further into the cause-effect, symptom-aetiology-cure stance. Here people seemed to accentuate drive theory and mechanics reminiscent of biology, and to leave by the wayside such concepts as narrative, resonance, and myth. At the same time, notably in the English independent movement and in France, the more pragmatic existentialist stance was embraced. In this view, one is saying, in effect, "no matter what DMS-IV may prescribe as a psychic symptomatology, there will never be a cookery book of psychoanalysis". Each psychoanalysis is treated as a fresh, new phenomenon, and is uniquely exploratory. Dr Michael Fitzgerald in Ireland went so far as to say in effect that each new psychoanalytic case has the potential of adding to the body of psychoanalytic knowledge.

There can be no doubt that this kind of humility — dare I say scientific humility? — must be necessary for any realistic or effective approach to the Other, to the real thing out there which will never be 100 per cent represented by any description, mathematical, intellectual, or even poetic. It is a typically human conceit to assume an equivalence between model and the reality. And in psychoanalysis, such existential humility in my view must characterise both our clinical work *and* our theoretical building. Even our metapsychological structures must be tentative and always recognised as only a part of the truth.

A Platonic Perspective

In the early psychoanalytic movement in Ireland, however, another psychoanalytic perspective emerged quite early on, a perspective which I would call Platonic. The early analysts in Ireland, led by Jonathan Hanaghan, certainly embraced an existential humility in their clinical practice. But the metapsychological outlook of this group was influenced by siting the raw data of psychoanalysis within a sort of Platonic framework. The clinical repercussions of this seem significant. To get the flavour of the Platonic outlook, it may be helpful to look not only at Plato, but at Zoroaster, who preceded him and at Jesus of Nazareth who came later. Although Jesus and Zoroaster are obviously well-known as religious figures, it is the philosophical content of their outlook which we will examine here, and which seems to form a continuous progression.

Zoroaster's views are hard to separate from those of his followers. Yet two main concepts stand out. First of all, it seems clear that he regarded the here-and-now world as a moment-by-moment projection of the underlying struggle between the forces of light and the forces of darkness. The forces of light were personified in Ahura Mazda, later contracted into "Ohrmazd". Although the Japanese car brand name may have other etymological roots, certainly the "Mazda" family of electric light bulbs manufactured by General Electric in America have a Zoroastrian god of light as their inspiration. Ahura Mazda's dark opponent is Ahriman. Their struggle is extramundane, in a higher plane of being; and the universe as we know it is a moment-by-moment projection of this more fundamental struggle, possibly in the way that a score card summarises actual struggles between actual people in the field of play. Or, in another metaphor, our "real" world is like the dance of light and shadow on a cottage wall, when the only source of illumination is the sputtering fire. The light-and-dark flickering (like our "real" world) only *represents* the process of chemistry and temperature in the hearth (like the Ahura Mazda/Ahriman struggle): a more fundamental reality. But Ahura Mazda is the ultimate creator, even of Ahriman, in the same way that Lucifer was seen by the Hebrews as a fallen angel.

A second key Zoroastrian idea is the notion of the "beneficent immortals" or Amesha Spentas, who dwell in this more
fundamental realm. There are seven of these, and they are
"Holy Spirit", "Justice and Truth", "Righteous Thinking", "Devotion", "Desirable Dominion", "Wholeness", and "Immortal-
ity". An individual can improve himself by getting more in tune
with these beneficent immortals, and so participate more effectively in the extramundane struggle between light and darkness, between Ahura Mazda and Ahriman.

Modern Western dating accepts the Zoroastrian tradition, and
places Zoroaster's adult life in the first half of the sixth century
BC. Almost exactly two hundred years later, and several hundred miles to the west, we have Plato in his dialogues summing
up the work of his mentor Socrates, and later adding to it. Socrates did not believe in writing things down, seeing the person-to-
person encounter as the only important matter to pursue, so that
Plato is the main source of insight into Socratic thought. Modern
scholars struggle to establish how much is Socrates, how much is
Socrates-interpreted-by-Plato, and how much is Plato's add-on.
But in Platonic thinking, three principles stand out:

1. *The Theory of Forms*, which has as it foundations the assumption that beyond the world of physical things there is a
   higher, spiritual realm of Forms or Ideas, such as the Forms
   of Beauty or Justice.

2. *This world*: in consequence, the things of this world are only
   imperfect copies of the Forms.

3. *Knowledge as recollection*: the notion that acquiring a profound understanding of the world is really just remembering
   what we already knew, before we were born; this implies the
   soul is not only eternal but pre-existent. In other words, before we were born, we dwelt in the realm of the Forms.

There is a clear parallel between these elements of Platonic
thought, and the prior conceptions of Zoroaster. Perhaps this
continuity can best be expressed in a chart.

Zoroaster	Plato
1. The Amesha Spentas	1. The Forms
2. (The realm of the Amesha Spentas)	2. The "higher spiritual realm of the Forms"
3. The world as a battlefield, or projection, of the vast struggle between Ahura Mazda and Ahriman.	3. This world as consisting of "imperfect copies of the Forms"
4. The final victory of Ahura Mazda and the universality of the "Desirable Dominion"	4. The Republic as the realisation in this world of relating and being according to the Forms.

This continuity may be a real one, based entirely on cultural diffusion: thinkers known to Socrates and Plato may have been directly or indirectly under the influence of Zoroastrian thought. If we assume, however, that this way of seeing things corresponds to a reality rather than a phantasy, or an intellectual construct, then the cultural diffusion may have been secondary to a gradually improving, or changing, direct perception of that objective reality. In Platonic terms, individuals like Zoroaster, Socrates, and Plato may be glimpsing the *same objective reality* through gradually clearing, or shifting, mists of forgetfulness. One important development in these elements going from Zoroaster to Plato is that the Zoroastrian system is partly dualistic — light vs. darkness — whereas the Platonic system sees us in our "reality" groping toward the Forms from our mundane position of forgetfulness and imperfection.

Another four hundred years later, and just south of a line between Zoroaster and Plato, we find Jesus of Nazareth. He is urging people to repent, to let go of old passions obsessively pursued; he affirms that the Kingdom of God is at hand, or somehow contactable. He instructs people to pray, ". . . thy Kingdom come, thy will be done, on earth as it is in heaven . . ." Jesus seems to acknowledge Plato's "forgetfulness" and to anticipate Freud's unconsciousness, when he prays for his oppressors, "Forgive them . . . for they know not what they do".

HANAGHAN'S PLATONIC VERSION OF PSYCHOANALYSIS

The Metaphysical Self

Jonathan Hanaghan was a sincere Christian, not adhering to any particular religious organisation, but seeing Jesus as urging his followers to get in touch with an invisible, extramundane kingdom of values: a view which I consider Platonic. This being so, Hanaghan did not see utopian yearnings in adults as being merely reflections on the lost ecstasy of breast-feeding times, or compensations for the lost sense of omnipotence, or the lost oceanic merging with the mother, *although all these things may also be true*. Taking his Platonic stand, Hanaghan sees us as having been with God before birth, so that our mother is the first transference figure. Her ministrations must fail in comparison to our premundane situation, so that we are bound to be shocked by our mother's shortcomings, which can range from difficult to catastrophic. To the extent that shortcomings in early maternal care — and later in the Oedipus development — are traumatic, psychoanalysis can help us untie the knots verbal and preverbal which involve splitting and (for later material) repression. But all our parents have failed us, compared to the perfect divine love we knew. Therefore, having passed through anger towards our parents for our ordeal, we can gradually learn to let go of our claims and forgive the poor figures that were our parents, who often as not did their best according to the knowledge and insights they had in their time. This is not a prescribed path, but a path many have followed to relative wholesomeness and strength. Using a religious term, Hanaghan sees this as perhaps the only realistic, effective form of *repentance* or letting-go.

This kind of Platonic/psychoanalytic thinking has important implications in several areas. These include Hanaghan's concept of the self; his view of moral and pseudomoral agencies in the unconscious mind; his notion of the child in the family; and his idea of the individual embedded in evolution and contributing to it. There are natural knock-on effects in clinical attitudes and practice. In German, Freud's mother tongue, "the ego" is not Latinised as in English, but is simply "das ich". Perhaps the classical affectation of the translators has done English-speaking psychoanalysis a favour, because unlike other languages (in French it is "le moi"), the English version of "the ego" does *not* imply that this mental agency is coextensive with oneself or one's self.

In any case, Hanaghan with his Platonic view of the pre-mundane existence of the self, sees *the self as quite distinct from the ego*. The foundation of the individual ego results from giving the self an individual genetic inheritance — with superego elements as well as instinctual patterning — and then immersing this self in spacetime, and in a specific human society, with its language, customs and institutions. The ego seen broadly is a set of organisational structures developed by the individual baby to cope with all the bewildering hassles of spacetime existence (waiting, moving, grasping, feeling pain, etc.) as well as with negotiating solutions to problems resulting from the existential three-way bind in which it finds itself (coping with tumultuous raw emotions, superego terrors, and parental deficiencies).

The metaphysical self is the inheritor, the possessor of the body-mind organism, including the ego, the id, and the superego. As the possessor of the organism, it is capable of choice, and exercises the power of choice. In the typical adult, neurotic individual, most of our decisions are made unconsciously. To the extent that we have been traumatised, our decisions can seem compulsive — indeed, can be compulsive for all practical purposes. The utility of psychoanalysis here is to help us, by broadening conscious access into the unconscious, to enlarge our possibility of choice.

The Temptation Situation

When we can access that level at which we are deciding, we face the *temptation situation*: Hanaghan again chooses the traditional religious term, but uses it in a carefully perceived psychoanalytic context. Whereas Freud saw some kind of quantity of excitation *causing* us to choose A or B, Hanaghan in my view focuses the microscope more closely. When we are facing, for example, the choice of repeating a destructive pattern, or of transcending it, Hanaghan asks us to look carefully at our experience of this moment. First there is a shapeless urge, not yet formed into a wish. Then we reply by forming our personal wish-fulfilment phantasy, our choice being influenced by our personal history of coping, and doubtless by hereditary factors as well. In a third movement, we can decide to act-out, if we choose to repeat the pattern. But during these steps of temptation, impulse pressure as a Freudian quantum is experienced by us in a two-fold fashion:

- *An increase in discomfort,* like an itch we can't scratch; and

- Once we have formed our answering phantasy, by an *increase in image presentation frequency* (our wish flashes more often, as if being fulfilled).

If we decide to say "no" to the repetition impulse, we can do so at either level, by enduring the discomfort and, if it has gone that far, by receiving in inaction the act-out phantasy flashes. In this way the metaphysical self can develop the power to exercise choice. Incidentally, once firm decision is made, both the discomfort and the image-presentation gradually fade away.

Moral and Pseudomoral Agencies

The Platonic view of a world of values to which we can gain access implies that in normal development we should witness the emergence of a mental agency whose function it is to perceive the aesthetic and the true. To this agency Hanaghan gave a name unfortunately used differently by other psychoanalytic theorists: the *ego-ideal.* In Hanaghan's use it means primarily this window on eternity, this faculty to see into the realm of truth and beauty. To Hanaghan, the experience of the ego-ideal in operation is not characterised by angry internal shouts, nor internal fear or guilt or dread. Nor again by alluring images of garish colour. The ego-ideal entices by a quiet sense of excellence; Hanaghan often used the Quaker term of the "still, small voice".

Because of the very quiet of it, this ego-ideal is often eclipsed or drowned out by the shouts, the anxieties, or the guilt-trips of the harsh super-ego. "Do you think that fear of punishment is a proper source of moral insight?" one of Hanaghan's friends asked a father who advocated child beating. This, in Hanaghan's view, is the nub of it. The shouting, intimidating, or bullying voice of our harsh superego is the voice of tribal or family taboo, which can only accidentally and only sometimes be accurate as a moral guide. Whilst in the *normal* development, exercise and practice in the use of the ego-ideal promotes personal growth, independence, and strength — the harsh superego in contrast is regularly, particularly in its more bizarre forms, associated with such mental disturbances as obsessional neurosis, hysteria, paranoia, and depression. The ego-ideal, as an ever surer moral and aesthetic guide, works towards integration of all the facets of the personality, whilst the pseudomoral agencies, such as the harsh superego, or even the sweetness of regressive phantasy, only express the interest of one or the other facet of the personality. The ego-ideal in particular is important in its role of informing us about good identification figures, thus promoting growth of the benign superego and the ego.

D.W. Winnicott wrote that "there is an early history of the superego in each individual; the introjects may (later) become human and father-like; but in earlier stages the superego introjects, used for control of id-impulses and id-products, are sub-human, and indeed are primitive to any degree". This proto-superego is particularly evident in paranoia and schizophrenia, but may also appear in lesser afflictions. One has the impression of many of the proto-superego elements, which seem clearly hereditary in many cases, that they call by taboo-curses for the *suppression* rather than the *channeling* of the id-impulses. This is of course a pathogenic role.

Yet many in the psychoanalytic world still see the superego as a continuum, benign at one end, harsh on the other. It seems clear to me that there are two distinct structures: the benign superego resulting from operation of the ego-ideal, and from benign parenting; and the harsh superego proceeding from the phylogenetic taboo-material and from the identification with harsh, attacking parents acting under the dominance of their own superego and of cultural taboos.

Aesthetic and moral awareness gradually superseding the intensities of the harsh superego: this is a hallmark of a healthy, wholesomely developed personality, and indeed an absolute necessity. The Platonic formulation of psychoanalytic theory makes a major contribution here. Clinically, when we see our client, immersed in psychotic struggles, beginning to have flashes of aesthetic appreciation, we become more hopeful of a successful outcome.

Myth of the Birth of the Hero

If we proceed into spacetime from elsewhere — "trailing clouds of glory", as Hanaghan describes it, quoting William Wordsworth — disappointment and disillusion are inevitable. This conception resonates well with the observed fact of children generally entertaining what Otto Rank called the *Myth of the Birth of the Hero*. In this imagining, the child reckons in its alienation that it is of royal birth, and is temporarily parked with these crass and often cruel step-parents. "One day", the myth continues, "my real destiny will appear, and I shall be recognised by one and all as possessing my real, royal family connections."

Hanaghan interprets this myth as a kind of shortsightedness. The child aims as high as it can see in selecting its royal origins. If our education and child-rearing were better, argues Hanaghan, the child would be more in touch with its real divine excellence and its real divine origin, and would not later be so likely to fall into shallow social snobbery.

Reversal of the Self-Preservation Instinct

Next, if our entry into the actual world is, as described by Hanaghan, part of our ego-development — doubtless appropriate for this stage of our evolutionary development — consists of what Hanaghan calls the *reversal of the self-preservation instinct*. Put at its simplest, the widespread presence of family environments actually *hostile* to children, and the lack very generally of what Winnicott called a facilitating environment, forces children to defend themselves outwardly and inwardly, with the emergence of what Wilhelm Reich called character-armour. This, according to Hanaghan, is a reversal of the self-preservation instinct, which in its true form would find survival value in being absolutely trusting. In short, our societies of today just are not up to it, and we force children by-and-large to defend themselves against us, and against their impulses which would provoke harsh responses from us.

The Cry of the Infant

Hanaghan accepted Freud's insight that the human infant is born prematurely, in comparison with other mammals. The colt or the calf can walk within hours or even minutes of birth; but walking for the human infant is an accomplishment of the 11- to 13-month old. The year of infantile helplessness is pregnant with consequences. In the first place, our close mammalian cousins communicate mainly through body language. Picture the dog with its lead in its mouth, cocking its head: who would miss this message, "Are we going for a walk? Please?" Such co-ordination is impossible for the human infant; it can only cry. It is not farfetched to see language, the hallmark of humanity, as an outgrowth of the year of helplessness.

Melanie Klein and her followers, perhaps to be seen in parallel with Alice Miller's more recent work, saw the infant's phantasies of grandiosity (infantile omnipotence) counterposed against its actual tininess and helplessness. In Kleinian psychoanalysis acceptance of this helplessness is a major achievement: an individual Copernican Revolution. But illuminating the modality of this acceptance was the contribution of Donald Winnicott, with his concept of the transitional object. According to him, in the time of helplessness the infant adopts a transitional object, reminiscent in odour or texture of mother, as a substitute to bridge the gaps when she was not there. (Freud foreshadowed this in his remarks about an infant playing with, or practising separation, with the *"fort-da"* game: the infant throwing away the spool, with its string attached, "gone!"; then hauling it back "here!") This in Winnicott's eyes is the genesis of symbolism, which contributes to language with its "signifiers" and "signified". But Winnicott goes further, to declare that all of human culture — our houses, clothes, cars, music, technology, central heating, poetry, etc. — serves a parallel function, and is an outgrowth of the humble security blanket.

Hanaghan's approach is similar:

The cry of the infant is immensely powerful; what other force could induce a young man and a young woman to devote two decades of their lives to caring for a fellow creature?

But Hanaghan, too, goes further. The cry of the infant, in evoking hitherto unexperienced powers of loyalty and determination in the young parents, has the potential of bringing into being what he called the beloved community: a beachhead into spacetime of the kingdom of heaven.

The Fall of Creation

The general presence in all creatures of the reversal of the self-preservation instinct, argues Hanaghan, is a sign of some cataclysmic, premundane fall of all life, possibly all creation. This may be viewed as an extension of Freud's "ontogeny replicates phylogeny" principle (and an extension of the notion of an individual Copernican Revolution). The infant's fall in reversing its self-preservation instinct is an echo of that premundane fall just as surely as energy bursts picked up by radio telescopes can be distant echoes of the primordial Big Bang. Yet slow progress in working towards a more caring society is the way we are going, and is in fact the way home. In this process, individual decisions, even on apparently trivial matters, can have cosmic or even trans-cosmic significance. In this sense, psychoanalytic assistance to individuals in learning to exercise their ego-ideal can have importance far beyond the life of this individual.

Cautionary Notes

Two notes seem to apply here. Firstly, this view of Hanaghan's Platonic outlook in psychoanalysis is necessarily incomplete. For Hanaghan, like Socrates, was dead set against writing things down. Again like Socrates, he felt that the person-to-person contact was meaningful, and produced very real and quite important results. In contrast the written word was not a dialogue, but a one-directional broadcast. It was only the persistent urging of his early colleagues that induced Hanaghan to write his two books: *Society, Evolution and Revelation*; and *Freud and Jesus*. These books are aimed at a general audience, rather than at analysts and therapists.

It is only by knowing Hanaghan personally, by reading and listening to many dozens of his talks, that this summary of his Platonic outlook could be prepared. The connecting logic is as perceived by myself, and will therefore necessarily be incomplete, a thin slice of a much larger, more intricately inwoven, and yet very substantially self-consistent picture involved over several decades by a group of excellent men and women, led by Hanaghan.

The other note concerns Hanaghan's style. In enunciating these ideals, Hanaghan is not playing guru, and is seldom prescriptive. The way he would put his point is experimental. In essence, he is saying, "I found it be this way in my own inner self-exploration. Why don't you have a look in yourself, and see if it is similar for you?"

SOME CONCLUSIONS

It is clearly a dangerous idea to shoehorn psychoanalysis into any ideology. Some colleagues find the medical models at times useful: forces mischanneled, libido transformations — all these are useful at times. Certainly the existential approach in clinical exploration is in fact more scientifically correct than a constricting "scientific" orthodoxy. Yet the Platonic underpinning to psychoanalysis, as developed by Hanaghan and his colleagues over several decades, has enriched the practice of those who adopt this approach, in several ways.

The concept of the metaphysical person, often trapped in his or her own defences, has at times enabled real improvement of individuals who would elsewhere be considered unsuitable for treatment. I can attest to this from my own practice, and from the practices of colleagues past and present. A key feature is keeping somehow in touch with that *person* behind all the barricades. In particular, it is important to note that paranoia and schizophrenia are *secondary* phenomena. The *retreat* to the paranoid-schizoid position, as discovered by Melanie Klein, therefore, *does not imply the dissolution of the self*. The self is just hiding. In the same way, those of us who deal with severely depressed people must not, in the end, be surprised if the client seems existentially to insist on a redesign of the universe as a precondition to getting better. If the ideas of Platonic psychoanalysis have any merit, this attitude is not unreasonable — merely impractical!

Reflecting, and at times interpreting, ego-ideal material can enhance ego-growth, as well as the burgeoning aesthetic perception of the individual. This is very crucial, more so then perhaps generally realised, replacing defective maternal mirroring.

Persistent and stubborn attention to mapping out the superego seems often to weaken the harsh, pathogenic structures, and to free up the ego-ideal development along with a sense of play and fun, considered so important by Winnicott. "Whose (accusing, mocking, attacking, scornful) voice is that?" is a question often asked. Pre-speech superego patterns can be equally significant, and these are generally played out in the transference.

Quite important, too, are techniques (launched by Freud at the time of his Wolf Man case and further developed later) for recognising and highlighting phylogenetic phantasies and their harsh superego content.

Once one's dark phantasies have been acknowledged, one's harsh superego partly rolled back, one's ego-ideal growth and aesthetic perception enhanced — then one arrives at a position considered important by Hanaghan. Here one begins to see parents and other significant early figures in a more realistic light. Those that were tyrants or oppressors may now be seen as tormented individuals, or people otherwise deprived, who were unable to relate properly. And often a sense of pity or compassion is then evoked, a part of a new forth-flowing, or forth-giving towards those early figures. Hanaghan again here used a religious term "forgiving", equating it to "forth-giving". Ability to forgive then becomes an important criterion of progress of the analysand. These steps must be arrived at by the client spontaneously — not prescribed by the analyst.

Finally, we have the issue of transference and counter-transference. In Platonic analysis, the analyst, buttressed by ongoing supervision, and/or by regular meetings with colleagues at which case-material is discussed, must receive a hell of a lot of negative transference. "This process isn't going anywhere"; "You've wrecked my life"; "Your lamp is terrible, if it was mine, I'd burn it"; "Your feet are horrible; no wonder you never got married" (to a female colleague): these are typical examples of the negative transference. They must be borne without counterattack, even by immediate "analysis" of the negative transference — although we might some time later politely disagree. And of course, all these attacks have a *kernel of truth*, which at some point later should be acknowledged. In this way, by receiving this "Beta" material, processing it in the Bion way into "Alpha" material, we are enabling the introjection into the client's psyche of the calm, reasonable analyst, and helping, all unseen, the development of the client's benign superego, self-respect, self-confidence, and ability to survive setbacks and attacks.

What then are the pros and cons? Is there any reality to this philosophical view, involving an extramundane realm of values, the metaphysical self, and Hanaghan's ego-ideal? From my own practice, here are some of the pros:

- The concept of the metaphysical self has helped me immensely with psychotic clients, especially people suffering from paranoia and from schizoid influences.

- In virtually all of my cases of psychosis or borderline disorders, a burgeoning aesthetic appreciation preceded or accompanied important improvements.

- Studies over the last ten to fifteen years, involving ultrasonic observation of infants *in utero*, have presented a pretty convincing picture that the foetus is not in a uterine Nirvana, but in an existence often fraught with anxiety or distress. Mother's moods produce hormonal discharges which enter the infant's blood and induce frighteningly powerful emotional responses in the infant. What is the hormonal signature of hate: adrenalin plus what? There has been evidence from several of my clients that they were passionately unwanted during pregnancy, and that the embryo understood this in a pre-speech certainty. Moreover twins vie remorselessly for *lebensraum* — apparently not Hitler's invention after all! But if the intrauterine world is fraught with terror and upsets, like later life in the outside world, where do the apparently ubiquitous dreams originate of a realm where everything is all right, where rules are wise and just, and governance is based on kindness and love?

In contrast to this rich supporting evidence, I can only find two contraindications:

- The Hanaghan views offend against defensively elaborated beliefs based on materialist philosophies rooted in Cartesian "extended substance" whilst ignoring Descartes's "non-extended substance".

- The Hanaghan views may not be politically correct in many schools of psychoanalysis.

In short, if the Hanaghan views are not correct, I am convinced that something rather like them must be.

Any analyst or therapist must, in my view, be existential in one's clinical approach. The old medical models remain at times useful. Hanaghan's Platonic approach seems important in helping individuals discover, or recover, their sense of beauty and their sense of direction based on that beauty: absolutely essential attributes for a healthy psychic whole. The approach seems also to enhance recovery and /or discovery of a wholesome spirit of adventure, often playful, no longer chained by neurotic anxiety and guilt.

In closing, perhaps it would be appropriate to quote the poetic vision of a nineteenth-century American Jewish socialist, Felix Adler:

> Sing we of the Golden City
> Pictured in the legends old:
> Everlasting light shines o'er it;
> Wondrous tales of it are told.
> Only righteous men and women
> Dwell within its gleaming walls.
> Wrong is banished from its borders;
> Justice reigns throughout its halls.

We are builders of that City.
All our joys and all our groans
Help to rear its shining ramparts;
All our lives are building stones.
For that City we must labour,
For its sake bear pain and grief;
In it find the end of living
And the anchor of belief.

And the work that we have builded
Oft with bleeding hands and tears,
Oft in error, oft in anguish,
Will not perish with our years.
It will last, and shine transfigured
In the final reign of right;
It will pass into the splendours
Of the City of the Light.

Chapter 5

RE-IMAGINING GOD

Richard Kearney

I come in the little things, saith the Lord — Evelyn Underhill

The divine, if it exists, exists not just for itself but for us. And the manner in which God comes to us, comes to mind, comes to be and to dwell as flesh amongst us, is deeply informed by the manner in which we think about God — in short, how we interpret, narrate and imagine God. This, I suggest, calls for a philosophical hermeneutics instructed by the various and essential ways in which God "appears" to us in and through "phenomena" and "signals" to us in and through "signs". It is my wager in this essay that one of the main ways in which the infinite comes to be experienced and imagined by our finite minds is as *possibility* — the ability to be. Even, and especially, when such possibility seems impossible to us.

I will proceed by means of three concentric circles — *scriptural*, *testimonial* and *literary*. Traversing this threefold "variation of imagination", I hope to identify some key characteristics of the God of the Possible as it reveals itself to us poetically.

THE SCRIPTURAL CIRCLE

My efforts to rethink God as *posse* draw primarily from the biblical message that what is impossible for us is possible for God. This latter notion of messianic possibility is evident in many Scriptural passages. In Mark 10, for example, we are told that while entry to the Kingdom seems impossible for humans, all things are made possible by God. The exact text reads: "For humans it is impossible but not for God; because for God everything is possible" (*panta gar dunata para to theo*) (Mark 10. 27). In similar vein, we are told in St John's Prologue that our ability to become sons of God in the Kingdom is something made possible by God: "Light shone in darkness and to all who received it was given the possibility (*dunamis*) to become sons of God". The term *dunamis* is crucial and can be translated either as power or possibility — a semantic ambivalence to which we shall return below. Further evocations of the possibilising power (*dunamis pneumatos*) of the Spirit are evidenced in Paul's letters to the Corinthians and Romans; but perhaps most dramatically of all in the Annunciation scene where Mary is told by the angel that the "*dunamis*" of God will overshadow her and that she will bear the son of God — "for nothing is impossible (*a-dunaton*) with God"(Luke 1).

In all these examples, divinity — as Father, Son or Spirit — is described as a possibilising of divine love and logos in the order of human history where it would otherwise have been impossible. In other words, the divine reveals itself here as the possibility of the kingdom — or if you prefer to cite a via negativa, as the *impossibility of impossibility*.

A hermeneutical poetics of the kingdom looks to some of the recurring *figures* — metaphors, parables, images, symbols — deployed in the Gospels to communicate the eschatological promise. The first thing one notes is that these figures almost invariably refer to a God of "small things" — to borrow from the wonderful title of Arundhati Roy's novel. Not only do we have the association of the Kingdom with the vulnerable openness and trust of "little children", as in the Matthew 10 passage cited above, but we also have the images of the yeast in the flour (Luke 13), the tiny pearl of invaluable price (Matt 13), and perhaps most suggestive and telling of all, the mustard seed (Mark 4) — a miniscule grain that blooms and flourishes into a capacious tree. The kingdom of God, this last text tells us, is "like a mustard seed that, when it is sown in the ground, is the smallest of all the seeds on the earth. But once it is sown, it springs up and becomes the largest of plants and puts forth large branches, so that the birds of the sky can dwell in its shade".

One might be tempted to call this recurring motif of the kingdom as the last or least or littlest of things — a *micro-theology* to the extent that it resists the standard macro-theology of the Kingdom as emblem of sovereignty, omnipotence and ecclesiastical triumph. The frequent reference in the Gospel to the judgment of the Kingdom being related to how we respond in history, here and now, to the "least of these" (*elachistos*) (e.g. Matt 25.40), is crucial. The loving renunciation of absolute power by Christ's empyting (*kenosis*) of the Godhead, so as to assume the most humble form of humanity (the last and least of beings), is echoed by the eschatological reminder that it is easier for the defenceless and powerless to enter the Kingdom than the rich and mighty. And I think it is telling — as Dostoyevsky reminds us in the Grand Inquisitor episode of the *Brothers Karamazov* — that the greatest temptation that Christ must overcome, after his forty days in the desert, is the will to become master and possessor of the universe. This is a temptation he faces again and again right up to his transfiguration on Mt Thabor when his disciples want to apotheosise and crown him by building a cult temple there on the mountain (Luke 9). Instead, Christ proceeds to a second kenotic act of giving, refusing the short route to immediate triumph and embracing the *via crucis* which demonstrates what it means for the seed to die before it is reborn as a flowering tree which hosts all living creatures. As "King", he enters Jerusalem not with conquering armies but "seated upon an ass's colt" (John 12). He upturns the inherited hierarchies of power, fulfilling the prophecy of Isaiah that he would bring justice to the world, not by "shouting aloud in the street" but as a "bruised reed that shall not break, a smoldering wick that shall not quench" (Isaiah 42:1-4).

But in addition to these *spatial* metaphors of the Kingdom exemplified by little things — yeast, a mustard seed, a pearl, a reed, an infant, the "least of these" — a hermeneutic poetics of the Kingdom might also look to the *temporal* figures of eschatology. These invariably take the form of a certain *achronicity*. I am thinking here of the numerous references to the fact that even though the Kingdom has *already come* — and is incarnate *here and now* in the loving gestures of Christ and all those who give, or receive, a cup of water — it still always remains a possibility *yet to come*. This is what Emanuel Levinas calls the "paradox of posterior anteriority"; and it is cogently illustrated in an aphorism of Walter Benjamin which combines the spatial figure of the portal with the eschatological figure of futurity: "This future does not correspond to homogenous empty time; because at the heart of every moment of the future is contained the little door through which the Messiah may enter."[1]

As "eternal", the kingdom transcends all chronologies of time. Christ indicates this when he affirms that "before Abraham was, I am" (John 8, 58), and when he promises a Second Coming when he will return again. In short, the Kingdom is both a) *already* there as historical possibility and b) *not yet* there as historically realised kingdom "come on earth". This is why we choose to translate the canonical theophany of God to Moses on Mt Sinai (*esher ayeh esher*) not as "I am who am" (*ego sum qui sum*) but as: "I am who may be". God is saying something like this: I will show up as promised but I cannot *be* in time and history, I cannot become fully embodied in the flesh of the world, unless you show up and answer my call "Where are you?" with the response "Here I am". (I explore this eschatological enigma of time in further detail in the conclusion below.)

THE TESTIMONIAL CIRCLE

Our second hermeneutic circle explores a poetics of the kingdom in light of a number of testimonies recorded by religious writers down through the ages. This we might call the *testimonial* or *confessional* genre. Unlike "metaphysical" thinkers who presuppose an ontological priority of actuality over possibility, these more "poetical" minds reverse the traditional priority and point to a new category of possibility — divine possibility — *beyond* the traditional opposition between the possible and the impossible.

Let me begin with the pregnant maxim of Angelus Silesius: "God is possible as the more than impossible." Here Silesius — a German mystical thinker often cited by Heidegger and Derrida — points towards an eschatological notion of possibility which might be said to transcend the three conventional concepts of the possible: 1) as an epistemological category of modal logic, along with necessity and actuality (Kant); 2) as a substantialist category of *potentia* lacking its fulfilment as *actus* (Aristotle and the scholastics); and 3) as a rationalist category of *possibilitas* conceived as a represention of the mind (Leibniz and the idealists). All such categories fall within the old metaphysical dualism of possibility versus impossibility. But Silesius intimates a new role for the possible as a ludic and liberal outpouring of divine play: "God is possible as the more than impossible. . . .God plays with Creation/All that is play that the deity gives itself/It has imagined the creature for its pleasure." Creation here is depicted as an endless giving of possibility which calls us toward the kingdom.

I think the early medieval Jewish commentator, Rashi, also had something like this in mind when he interprets Isaiah's God calling to his creatures — "I cannot be God unless you are my witnesses." He takes this to mean: "I am the God who will be whenever you bear witness to love and justice in the world."[2] And I believe that the Holocaust victim Etty Hillesum was gesturing towards a similar notion when, just weeks before her death in a concentration camp, she wrote: "You God cannot help us but we must help you and defend your dwelling place inside us to the last".[3] Both Rashi and Hillesum were witnessing to the *dunamis* of God as *the power of the powerless*. This, clearly, is not the imperial power of a sovereign; it is a dynamic call to love which possibilises and enables humans to transform their world — by giving itself to the "least of these", by empathising with the disinherited and the dispossessed, by refusing the path of might and violence, by transfiguring the mustard seed into the kingdom, each moment at a time, one act after an other, each step of the way. This is the path heralded by the Pauline God of "nothings and nobodies" (*ta me onta*) excluded from the triumphal pre-eminence of totality (*ta onta*) — a kenotic, self-emptying, crucified God whose "weakness is stronger than human strength" (I Corinthians 1:25). It signals the option for the poor, for non-violent resistance and revolution taken by peacemakers and dissenting "holy fools" from ancient to modern times. It is the message of suffering rather than doing evil, of loving one's adversaries, of "no enemies", of "soul force" (*sat-yagraha*). One thinks of a long heritage ranging from Isaiah, Jesus, Siddhartha and Socrates to such contemporary figures as Gandhi, Havel, Dorothy Day, Jean Vanier, Ernesto Cardinal, Tich Nhat Hahn and Martin Luther King, amongst others. The God witnessed here goes beyond the will-to-power.

Nicholas of Cusa, as already mentioned, offers some interesting insights into this eschatological God when he declares that "God alone is all he is able to be" (*Trialogus de Possest*).[4] Unlike the God of metaphysical omnipotence, underlying the perverse logic of theodicy which seeks to justify evil as part of the divine Will, this notion of God as an "abling to be" (*posse* or *possest*) points in a radically different direction. Let us pause for a moment to unpack the phrase, "God is all he is able to be". Since God is all good God is not able to be non-good, that is non-God — defect or evil. In other words, God is *not* omnipotent in the traditional metaphysical sense understood by Leibniz and Hegel. The Divine is not some being able to be all good *and* evil things. That is why God could not help Etty Hillesum and other victims of evil. God is not responsible for evil. And Hillesum understood this all too well when she turned the old hierarchies on their head and declared that it is *we* who must help God to be God.

Was Hillesum not in fact subscribing here to a long — if often neglected — biblical heritage? After all, if Elijah had not heard the "still small voice" of God in his cave, we would never have received the wisdom of his prophecy. If a young woman from Nazareth had said "no" to the angel of the annunciation, the Word would not have become Flesh. If certain fishermen, tax collectors and prostitutes had not heard the call to follow the Son of Man, there would have been no Son of God — and no Gospel witness. So too, if Hillesum and others like her had not let God be God by defending the divine dwelling place of *caritas* within them, even in those most hellish moments of holocaust horror, there would have been no measure of love — albeit it as tiny as the mustard seed — to defy the hate of the Gestapo. For if God's loving is indeed unconditional, the realisation of that loving *posse* in this world is conditional upon our response. If we are waiting for God, God is waiting for us. Waiting for us to say "yes", to hear the call and to act, to bear wit-

ness, to answer the *posse* with *esse*, to make the word flesh —
even in the darkest moments.

I think Dionysius the Areopagite could be said to add to our
understanding of this great enigma when he speaks, in Book 7
of the *Divine Names*, of a "possibility beyond being" (*hyper-
ousias dunameos*) which engenders our desire to live more
abundantly and seek the good. "Being itself", he writes, "only
has the possibility to be from the possibility beyond being."
And he adds that it is "from the infinitely good posse (*dunamis*)
of what it sends to them (that) they have received their power
(*dunamis*)".[5] I am tempted to relate this notion of an infinitely
good possibilising of God to another extraordinary passage in
the *Divine Names* — this time Book 9, section 3 — where Dionysius writes of the God of little things: "God is said to be small as
leaving every mass and distance behind and proceeding un-
hindered through all. Indeed the small is the cause of all the
elements, for you will find none of these that have not partici-
pated in the form of smallness. Thus, smallness is to be interpreted with respect to God as its wandering and operating in
all and through all without hindrance "penetrating down to the
division of the soul, spirit, joint and marrow", and discerning
thoughts and "intentions of the heart", and indeed of all beings.
"For there is no creation which is invisible to its face" (Heb 4,
12). This smallness is without quantity, without quality, without
restraint, unlimited, undefined, and all embracing although it is
unembraced".[6] Is this extraordinary passage by Dionysius not a
passionate invitation to embrace a micro-theology of the kingdom? Is it not a solicitation to embrace an eschatology of little
things — mustard seeds, grains of yeast, tiny pearls, cups of
water, infinitesimal everyday acts of love and witness? It appears so.

Moreover, I think it is just this kind of micro-theology that
Gerard Manley Hopkins had in mind when he records God's
grace in small and scattered epiphanies of the quotidian —
when he speaks, for example, of God's "pied beauty" being
manifest in various "dappled things", from "finches wings" and
"rose-moles all in stipple upon trout that swim" to "all things
counter, original, spare, strange;/Whatever is fickle, freckled
— who knows how?" (*Pied Beauty*). For Hopkins, it is not the

mighty and triumphant Monarch that epitomises the pearl of the kingdom ("immortal diamond") but, contrariwise, the court fool, the joker in the pack, the least and last of these. Here is Hopkins's take on the eschatological kingdom:

> In a flash, at a trumpet crash,
> I am all at once what Christ is, since he was what I am,
> And
> This Jack, Joke, poor potsherd, patch, matchwood,
> Immortal diamond,
> Is immortal diamond.

Hopkins' deity is one of transfiguration rather than coercion, of *posse* rather than power, of little rather than large things.[7] An echo perhaps of Dante's deity in the *Paradiso* who is described as a tiny, indivisible point of light in contrast to the towering figure of Lucifer in the final Canto of the *Inferno*. But in our shift of registers from theology to poetry we are already embarking on our next circle of readings.

THE LITERARY CIRCLE

In our third and final hermeneutic circle — the *literary* — I include a number of passages which offer more explicitly poetic epiphanies of the possible. This amplification of our investigation to embrace a literary poetics extends the range of reference to take in soundings of *posse* which transcend the confessional limits of theism or atheism, enjoying as they do a special liberty of imagination — a "poetic licence" to entertain an unlimited variation of experience. As Emily Dickinson rightly observed, "possibility is a fuse lit by imagination", a belief which informs her imaging of the eschatological possible:

> I dwell in possibility —
> A fairer house than prose —
> More numerous of windows —
> Superior — for doors . . .
> Of visitors — the fairest —
> For Occupation — This —
> The spreading wide my narrow Hands
> To gather Paradise —

The French author, Rabelais, had his eye on a similar paradise when he affirmed the possibility of life through death, yea-saying to his last moments as he jubilantly declared: *"J'avance vers le grand possible!"* In his remarkable novel, *Man without Qualities*, the Austrian writer Robert Musil offers a further perspective on the eschatological *posse* when he claims that "possibility is the dormant design of God in man" — a design waiting to be awakened by our poetic dwelling in the world. Our true vocation in history, for Musil, is one of utopian invention. It involves an audacious surpassing of given reality towards imagined possibility. Here is the passage in full:

> One might define the meaning of the possible as the faculty of thinking all that *might be* just as much as what is. . . .The implications of such a creative disposition are huge. . . The possible consists of much more than the dreams of neurasthenics; it also involves the still dormant plans of God. A possible event or truth is not just the real event or truth minus the "reality"; rather it signals something very divine, a flame, a burning, a will to construct a utopia which, far from fearing reality, treats it simply as a perpetual task and invention. The earth is not so spent, after all, and never has it seemed so fascinating.[8]

The metaphor of fire — with its allusions to both the burning bush (Exod 3:14) and the Pentecostal flame of speaking tongues — is also explored by Wallace Stevens in a poem addressed to the philosopher, George Santayana, entitled "To an Old Philosopher in Rome". Here again the correspondence between the simple (indigent, small, inconsequential) and the eschatological (the kingdom) is conveyed by the figure of a candle flame which illumines the real in the light of the "celestial possible". The pneumatological call to speak in tongues commits itself here to a poetics of the poor and unremembered. Stevens writes:

> A light on the candle tearing against the wick
> To join a hovering excellence, to escape
> From fire and be part of that of which
> Fire is the symbol: the celestial possible (. . .)
> Be orator but with an accurate tongue
> And without eloquence, O, half-asleep,

Of the pity that is the memorial of this room,
So that we feel, in this illumined large,
The veritable small (. . .)
Impatient for the grandeur that you need
In so much misery, and yet finding it
Only in misery, the afflatus of ruin,
Profound poetry of the poor...
It is poverty's speech that seeks us out the most.

But it is doubtless the Prague poet, Rainer Maria Rilke, who composes one of the most inspiring invocations of the gracious power of *posse* in the conclusion to his *Letters to a Young Poet.* Here the eschatological promise of a coming God is combined with the erotic expectancy of a waiting lover. "Why don't you think of him (God) as the one who is coming", he asks his youthful correspondent, as

> one who has been approaching from all eternity, the one who will someday arrive, the ultimate fruit of a tree whose leaves we are? What keeps you from projecting his birth into the ages that are coming into existence, and living your life as a painful and lovely day in the history of a great pregnancy? Don't you see how everything that happens is again and again a beginning, and couldn't it be *His* (God's) beginning, since, in itself, starting is always so beautiful?

Then Rilke poses this crucial question:

> If he is the most perfect one, must not what is less perfect *precede* him, so that he can choose himself out of fullness and superabundance? — Must not *he* be the last one, so that he can include everything in himself, and what meaning would we have if he whom we are longing for has already existed? As bees gather honey, so we collect what is sweetest out of all things and build Him.

Rilke ends this remarkable passage with a call to vigilant attention and expectancy. Messianism at its best. The metaphor of the flowering, flourishing mustard seed is brought to a new poetic intensity. "Be patient", Rilke counsels the young poet, "and realise that the least we can do is to make coming into existence no more difficult for Him (God) than the earth does for spring when it wants to come" (*Letters to a Young Poet*).[9]

Here we return, as it were, to the "pregnant sense of the possible" noted in our citation from Kierkegaard above — the interweaving of the divine and the human in patient prayer and longing. And this eschatological desire, as Rilke vividly reminds us, is not confined to human existence but involves, by extension, the entire expanse of the terrestrial universe as it awaits, yearns and prepares itself for the coming *prima vera*.

My daughter, who brought this passage to my attention, told me this was a God she could believe in! Could I disagree?

CONCLUSION

So much depends, then, on what we mean by the *possible*. If one defines possibility according to established convention as a category of modal logic or metaphysical calculus — then God is closer to the impossible than the possible. But if one seeks, as I do, to reinterpret the possible as eschatological *posse,* from a post-metaphysical poetical perspective, the stakes are very different. For now we are talking of a *second* possible (analogous to Ricoeur's "second naiveté") *beyond* the impossible, *otherwise* than impossible, *more* than impossible, at the *other side* of the old modal opposition between the possible and the impossible. And here we find ourselves closer to the Kierkegaard's "passion for the possible" as portal to faith.

I think it is crucial to recall here the telling distinction between two competing translations of the Greek term *dunamis*. On the one hand, we have the metaphysical rendering of the term as *potestas/potentia*, that is, as a potency understood in terms of an economy of power, causality, substance — what Levinas calls the economy of the Same (or Totality). On the other hand, we have an eschatological rendering of *dunamis* as *posse/possest*, that is, as a gracious and gratuitous giving which possibilises love and justice in this world. It is this later interpretation of *dunamis* that I have been seeking to promote in my three hermeneutic detours through the poetics of the possible (and, in more depth and detail in *The God who May Be*).

In triumphalist accounts of the kingdom, the advent of the Messiah on the last day is often described in militaristic terms — as sublimely apocalyptic rather than lovingly vulnerable, as

"almighty" rather than solicitous, as coercive rather than caring. By contrast, the divine *posse* I am sponsoring here is more
healing than judgmental, more disposed to accept the "least of
these" than to meet out punishment and glory. If God can prevent evil from happening by re-creating the historical past, as a
theologian like Peter Damian once suggested, He is by implica-
tion a God of theodicy: namely, a God who has the power to
decide whether history unfolds as good or evil. To me, this
sounds like *potestas* rather than *posse.* A far cry from the divine
power of the powerless which Etty Hillesum invokes when she
summons us to help God to be God in the face of violence and
war. A world away from the God of little things.

* * *

Sometimes I have been asked what would happen to the God of
the Possible if we were to destroy the earth? How can God's
promise of a kingdom on earth be fulfilled if there is no earth to
come back to? What might be said of the existence of God in
such a scenario? There are a few observations I would like to
make here by way of conclusion, surmises which claim the poetic licence of a "free imaginative variation"!

First, I would say that as eternally perduring and constant
(that is, as faithful and attentive to us in each *present moment*),
God would live on as an endless *promise* of love and justice.
This would be so even if we fail or frustrate this covenant by
denying its potential for historical fulfilment *on earth*. In this
case, God would be like a spouse abandoned by a spouse — to
take up the bride/bridegroom analogy from the Song of Songs.
A lover forsaken. Or to borrow a metaphor from Hildegard of
Bingen, the *posse* would be like a tree deprived of its greening
(*viriditas*).[10] If denied its ultimate incarnation in the last days,
the possible God would be like a flowering seed arrested before it could come to its full flourishing and fruition on the earth.
It would still be *adventurus*, but no longer *futurus*. The divine
advent would be deprived of an historical, human future but
would remain, in each moment, enduringly faithful in spite of
all. It would still be a "yes" in the face of our "no".

Second, as eternal *memory* (past), the divine *posse* would
preserve all those eschatological "moments" from the past

where the divine was incarnated in the flesh of the world every time (as Christ and Isaiah taught) someone gave a cup of cold water to someone else. In kairological as opposed to merely chronological time, these instants would be eternally "repeated" in divine remembrance. This would mark a re-jigging of the old adage: "The good that men do lives after them, the evil is interred with their bones"(to juggle with a line from Shakespeare's *Julius Caesar*). It would be in keeping with the repeated assurances of the biblical deity to remember the faithful who lived and died in history: e.g. Isaiah 49: 14-15: "Can a mother forget her infant, be without tenderness for the child of her womb? Even should she forget, I will never forget you". And it would also be consonant with the contrary commitment to erase the memory of evil: "The Lord is close to the broken hearted/The Lord confronts the evildoers/To destroy remembrance of them from the earth"(Psalm 34). There is then a deeply eschatological character to the biblical injunction to "remember"(*zakhor*). And this character is what translates God's mindfulness of creatures into a form of "anticipatory memory" (the term is Herbert Marcuse's) which preserves a future for the past. As Psalm 105 tells us, "He remembers forever his covenant which he made binding for a thousand generations — which he entered into with Abraham . . .". In other words, the promise made at the beginning of time is kept by the divine *posse* as an "eternal" remembrance of both the historical past and present right up to the *parousia*.

Thirdly and finally then, qua eternal *advent* (future), we might say that even though we would have deprived the divine *posse* of its future realisation as a kingdom *come on earth*, we could not, by such an act of self-destruction, deprive God of the possibility of starting over again. Nothing *good* is impossible to God. And rebirth in the face of death is good. As in any nuptial promise or pledge, each partner can speak for him/herself only: God can only promise for God, not for us. We are entirely free to break off *our* part of the promise at any time. And if we do, if we engage in collective self-destruction (God forbid!), why should God not have a "second chance"? Is not *posse*, after all, the possibility of endless beginning?

Of course, the *posse* of the kingdom is not just a promise for humanity as a universal community (to be reassembled as the mystical body of Christ on the last day, according to the Patristic notion of *anakephalaoisis*/Recapitulation). *Posse* is also and equally a promise for each unique self whose singular good — but not evil — will be preserved eternally in the recollection of the *deus adventurus:* like each glistening speck of dust in a comet's tail or each glint of plankton in the nocturnal wake of a ship. But if we destroy the earth we also refuse the possibility of each of these recollected and resurrected selves returning to a "new heaven as new earth" on the last day. They would return with *posse* — as eternal promise — but without the *esse* of a Second Coming.

*   *   *

Several of the above remarks and conjectures find textual support, I believe, in the "Palestinian formula" of eschatological memory (*eis anamnesin*) prevalent in late Jewish and early Christian literature. The formula finds one of its earliest inscriptions in Psalm 111, "the righteous will be for eternal remembrance"; and again in Psalms 37 and 69, where the memory of God refers not just to creatures remembering their Creator in rituals and liturgies but also to the Creator recalling creatures, making the past present before God in a sort of eternal re-presentation which endures into the future and beyond. Likewise in Ecclesiasticus we find the repeated prayer that God might mercifully remember his children. As the biblical commentator Joachim Jeremias observes, such remembrance is an "effecting and creating event which is constantly fulfilling the eschatological covenant promise. . . . When the sinner "is not to be remembered" at the resurrection, this means that he will have no part in it"(Ps Sol. 3.11). And when God no longer remembers sin, he forgets it (Jer 31.34; Heb 8.12; 10.17), this means that he forgives it. God's remembrance is always an action in mercy or judgment".[11]

The notion of eschatological memory is, as noted, also frequently witnessed in New Testament literature where it takes the form of a double "repetition" — looking to past and future simultaneously. In the Eucharistic formula — "do this in remembrance

of me"(*eis ten emen anamneisin*) (Luke 22.19; Paul I Cor 11.24) —
the proper translation of the repetition injunction, in keeping
with the Palestinian memorial formula, is this: "Do this so that
God may remember me".[12] The appeal to divine memory during
the Eucharistic sharing of bread and wine may be seen accordingly as an echo of the third benediction of the grace after Passover meal which asks *God to remember the Messiah* — a
benediction which is followed in turn with a petition for "the remembrance of all thy people": "may their remembrance come
before thee, for rescue, goodness . . .".[13] The remembrance of
past suffering is thus tied to the hope for the advent of the
parousia — for Jews the entry of the Messiah to Jerusalem, for
Christians the return of Christ on the last day. The petition for
repetition — in the *kairological* rather than *chronological* sense
— may be translated as: "God remembers the Messiah in that he
causes the kingdom to break in by the *parousia*."[14]

This allusion to a bi-lateral temporality whereby divine
memory recalls the *past as future* is further evidenced in Paul's
gloss on the Eucharistic remembrance formula: "For as often as
you eat this bread and drink this cup, you proclaim the Lord's
death *until he comes*" (*achri ou elthei*. See I Cor 11.23-25). Indeed the use of the subjunctive term *achri* refers often in the
New Testament to the arrival of the eschaton (Rom 11.25; I Cor
15.25; Luke 21.24). The crucial phrase here — "until he comes"
— may thus be read in light of the liturgical *maranatha* (come
lord!) invoked by the faithful in their prayers for the coming of
God. So rather than remembering the death of God as no more
than a historical event of the past, the remembrance formula
can be said to celebrate it as an eschatological advent — that is,
as the inauguration of a New Covenant. "This proclamation expresses the vicarious death of Jesus as the beginning of the salvation time and prays for the coming of the consummation. As
often as the death of the Lord is proclaimed at the Lord's supper, and the *maranatha* rises upwards, God is reminded of the
unfulfilled climax of the work of salvation "until (the goal is
reached, that) he comes. Paul has therefore understood the
anamnesis as the eschatological remembrance of God that is to
be realised in the *parousia*".[15] It is with this in mind that Luke
speaks of the eschatological jubilation and "gladness" (*agal-*

liasis) which characterises the mealtimes of the earliest Christian communities (Acts 2.46).

In sum, the close rapport between the Eucharistic request for repetition and the Passover ritual suggest that for both Judaism and Christianity the Kingdom advent is construed as a *retrieval-forward of the past as future*. The remembrance formula might be interpreted accordingly as something like this: "Keep gathering together in remembrance of me so that I will remember you by keeping my promise to bring about the consummation of love, justice and joy in the *parousia*. Help me to be God!". Or as the Coptic version of the formula goes: "May the Lord come . . . If any man is holy, let him come. *Maranatha*. Amen".

The above conjectures operate, for the most part, in the realm of hermeneutical poetics which enjoys a certain imaginative liberty vis-à-vis the strictures of theological dogma, speculative metaphysics or empirical physics. Though, I hasten to add, a fruitful dialogue remains open with all three disciplines.

* * *

Let me end with a final eschatological image from the poetics of the kingdom — the invitation to the feast. "I stand at the door and knock, says the Lord. If anyone hears my voice and opens the door, I will come in and sit down to supper with him, and he with me." The great thing about this promise of an eschatological banquet is that no one is excluded. The Post-God of *posse* knocks not just twice but a thousand times, nay, infinitely, ceaselessly, until there is no door unopened, no creature, however small or inconsequential, left out in the cold, hungry, thirsty, uncared for, unloved, unredeemed. The Post-God keeps knocking and calling and delivering the word until we open ourselves to the message and the letter becomes spirit, the word flesh. And what is this message? An invitation to the kingdom. And what is the kingdom? The kingdom is a cup of cold water given to the least of these; it is bread and fish and wine given to the famished and un-housed, a good meal and (we are promised) one hell of a good time lasting into the early hours of the morning. A morning that never ends.

Notes

[1] Walter Benjamin, "Theologico-Political Fragment" (1921) in *One Way Street*, NLB, London, 1979, pp. 155 f.

[2] Rashi, *The Torah: With Rashi's Commentary*, Mesorah Publications, New York, 1997. It would be interesting to relate Rashi's rabbinical interpretation with Isaac Luria's Kabbalist reading of God in terms of a generous withholding or "withdrawal" (*zimzum*) which invites human creatures to subsequently retrieve and reanimate the fragments of the "broken vessels" of divine love which lie scattered like tiny seeds throughout the created universe. This reading, which exerted a deep influence on Hassidic thinkers as well as on philosophers like Simone Weil, seems to confirm our own account of God's refusal to impose himself on creation — as some kind of omnipotent fulfilled being (*Ipsum Esse subsistens*), Sufficient Reason or Supreme Cause (*ens causa sui*) — preferring to relate to humans in the realm of the "possible" rather than the purely "actual" or "necessary". I am grateful to my Boston College colleague, Marty Cohen, for bringing the insights of the Lurianic Kabbala to my attention. See in particular his article, "Sarach's Harp" in *Parabola*, Fall 1997, Vol. 22, No 3.

[3] Etty Hillesum, *An Interrupted Life*, Owl Books, New York, 1996, p. 176.

[4] Nicholas of Cusa, *Trialogus de Possest* in *A Concise Introduction to the Philosophy of Nicholas of Cusa*, University of Minnesota Press, Minneapolis, 1980, p. 69. The original Latin reads: "Deus est omne id quod esse potest".

[5] Pseudo-Dionysius the Areopagite, *The Divine Names and Mystical Theology*, trans. J.D. Jones, Marquette University Press, Milwaukee, 1980, p. 182.

[6] *Ibid.*, p. 188. For a further exploration of the link between negative theology and our micro-eschatology see Stanislas Breton, *The Word and the Cross*, Fordham UP, New York, 2002, pp. 8-11, 49-50, 60-70, 80-91, 112-114. See in particular Breton's radical claim that we must give to God the being he has not, qua thirsting, kenotic, crucified stranger (pp. 121-122). The *dunamis* of God is here identified with the *germen nihili* or "power of nothing" which reveals itself as a "double nothingness" and powerless which liberates those oppressed by the power of *ta onta,* sowing the seed of non-being epitomised by the Beatitudes so that the eschatological tree of love and justice may flower and flourish (pp. 80–84 and *xxiv-xxvi*). For it is in and as a "seed of non-being" that, in Eckhart's resonant phrase, "God becomes verdant in all the honour of his being" (cited p. 80).

[7] See the illuminating reading of Hopkins in Mark Patrick Hederman, *Anchoring the Altar: Christianity and the Work of Art*, Veritas, Dublin, 2002, pp. 131f. It is important to note that this micro-theological emphasis on God as less rather than more is not confined to the Judeo-Christian tradition. It is also to be found in much of the Buddhist and Hindu wisdom literature, see for instance the following passage from Krishnamurti: "The silence which is not the silence of the ending of noise is only a small beginning. It is like going through a small hole to an enormous, wide, expansive ocean, to an immeasurable, timeless state" (*Freedom from the Known,* Harper, San Francisco, 1969, p. 109). Interestingly, one of the "siddhis", the powers that a yogi/yogini may acquire, is to become as small as an atom. Even Winnie the Pooh knows this, as in the following passage: "It is hard to be brave," said Piglet, sniffing slightly, "when you're only a Very Small Animal". Rabbit, who had begun to write very busily, looked up and said: "It is because you are a very small animal that you will be useful in the adventure before us".

[8] Rainer Maria Rilke, *Letters to a Young Poet*, trans. Stephen Mitchel, Vintage Books, 1986, pp. 61–63.

[9] *Ibid.* p. 63. The emphasis here on the earth as correspondent for divine eros highlights, once again, the incarnational tendency of theo-eroticism. The earth is full of the seeds of the divine (what Augustine, borrowing from the Stoics, called *logoi spermaticoi)*, incubating within the finite historical world like latent potencies waiting to be animated and actualised by the infinitely incoming grace of God as transcendent *posse.* If one removes transcendent *posse* from this equation, one relapses into a purely immanentist dialectic (evolutionary materialism or, at best, process theology). On the other hand, if one ignores the immanence of terrestrial and human potencies, one is left with an inordinately inaccessible and abstract deity — a sort of acosmic alterity without face or voice (e.g. deism or deconstruction). A hermeneutical poetics of divine *posse* tries to preserve a delicate balance between these opposite extremes.

[10] I am grateful to my wise friend and teacher, Peggy McLoughlin, for this reference and the quotes below. Here is one verse in which the term *viriditas* appears:

> O most noble greening power (*O nobilissima viriditas)*
> Rooted in the sun,
> Who shine in dazzling serenity
> In a sphere
> That no earthly excellence

Can comprehend.
You are enclosed
In the embrace of divine mysteries,
You blush like the dawn
And burn like a flame of the sun.

"For her, the energy that drives the universe — which she calls VIRID-ITAS, or the greening force — is also the power of the Living Light, which is Love-caritas. The expression of this in the creation is music. The original creation was a miracle of equilibrium, of perfect harmony, which the Fall disturbed; the incarnation restores a new harmony — indeed the Word of God is music itself, and the soul of mankind if symphonic: *symphonialis est anima.* . . . Here she finds the dynamic expression of the love of God and his promise to bring mankind back to him, the expression in the body of the green-growing grace of *viriditas*" (*Great Spirits 1000–2000: The Fifty-Two Christians who Most Influenced their Millennium,* ed by Selina O'Grady and John Wilkins, Paulist Press, New York, 2002.

[11] Joachim Jeremias, *The Eucharistic Words of Jesus,* Fortress Press, Philadelphia, 1977, p. 249. I am indebted to two of my colleagues at Boston College, Gary Gurtler and John Manoussakis, for bringing these comments and references by Dionysius and Jeremias to my attention.

[12] Jeremias, p. 252.

[13] *The Passover Haggadah,* Schocken Books, New York, 1953, p. 63.

[14] Jeremias, p. 252. One might see a repetition of the eschatological forgetting and remembering from the finite human perspective in Dante's *Divine Comedy* (Purgatory Canto 28) where the Pilgrim encounters the two inexhaustible streams of the garden, *Lethe* and *Eunoe,* of which the former washes away all memory of sin while the latter retrieves the memory of good deeds and life-giving moments.

[15] Jeremias, p. 253.

Chapter 6

PHILOSOPHISING THE GIFT:
AN INTERVIEW WITH RICHARD KEARNEY

Mark Manolopoulos

MM: In the Derrida/Marion debate "On the Gift" (Villanova, 1997) you ask the question "Is there a Christian philosophy of the gift?"[1] Do you think either Derrida or Marion or both provide handy directions? Could you summarise or interpret their insights? And whose argument do you find more persuasive?

RK: They did avoid the question. In Derrida's case that is logical because he will always — reasonably for a deconstructionist — try to avoid tying the messianicity of the gift to any messianism as such, be it Christian, Jewish, Islamic, or any other kind. So it makes sense for him not to engage in that debate *per se* because he would say: "That's beyond my competence. I'm not a Christian. 'I rightly pass for an atheist.'[2] I respect Christianity. I'm fascinated by their theological and philosophical expressions of the notion of the gift — I learn from it — but it's not my thing." Marion I find a little bit more perplexing in this regard because he *is* a Christian philosopher. He has talked about "eucharistic hermeneutics" in *God Without Being*.[3] Christ is a "saturated phenomenon" for Marion.[4] But Marion is going through a phase — and this was evident at the Villanova conference — where he doesn't want to be labeled as a "Christian philosopher" — and certainly *not* a Christian *theologian*. He wants to be a phenomenologist. So, being true — at least to some extent — to Husserl's

phenomenology as a universal science, he wants to be independent of presuppositions regarding this or that particular
theological revelation: Christian, Jewish, or otherwise. I think
that's why in his essays on "the saturated phenomenon", Marion
goes back to Kant. The Kantian sublime offers a way into the
saturated phenomenon, as does the notion of the gift or donation,
which — like Husserlian phenomenology — precedes the question of theological confessions and denominations. And I think
Marion wants to retreat to that position so that he won't be labeled a Christian apologist — which I think he is. I think he's a
Christian theologian who's trying to pretend he's not. Personally,
my own attempt to negotiate that would be to say that there's two
ways of doing phenomenology — and both are equally valid.
One is to begin with certain theological and religious presuppositions. The other is to do it operating a theological reduction,
where you say: "We're not going to raise theological issues
here." That's following the basic Husserlian and Heideggerian
line. In the *Introduction to Metaphysics* Heidegger says something like: "The answer to the question 'Why is there something
rather than nothing?' — if you fail to bracket out theology — is:
because God created the world."[5] But if you bracket it out you
don't begin with theological presuppositions — and that is what
Husserl does, what Heidegger does, and what Derrida does. I
think Marion mixes the two, although in the exchange with Derrida I think he's trying to get back to that kind of a *pure* phenomenology. He keeps saying: "I'm a phenomenologist! I'm
doing phenomenology!" Then there is the other way of doing
phenomenology *in dialogue with* theology, which doesn't
bracket it out but sort of half-suspends it. We might call this a
quasi-theological phenomenology or a quasi-phenomenological
theology. In other words, it acknowledges that there's a certain
hybridity, but it doesn't want to presuppose straight off which
comes *first*: the giving of the gift as a phenomenological event or
the divine creation of the world as source of all gifts. It allows for
a certain ambiguous intermeshing, intermixing, crossweaving or
chiasmic kind of interlacing (in Merleau-Ponty's sense). And it
seems to me that that's perfectly legitimate. Even though it's
methodologically more complex and more ambivalent than the
Husserlian move of saying "Bracket out all political, theological,

ideological, cultural presuppositions", it's actually truer to life because life *is* the natural attitude. And the natural attitude *is* infused with presuppositions. And it includes *both* (a) experiences of the gift as pure gift and (b) experiences of the gift for believers as coming from Yahweh or Christ or Allah or the Sun God/dess. And it seems to me that the phenomenology of unbracketed experience, the phenomenology of the natural attitude — which I think Merleau-Ponty gets pretty close to — is what I am practicing in *The God Who May Be*.[6] I'm not writing as a theologian because I don't have the theological competence. I'm writing as a philosopher, but one who, as a philosopher, feels quite entitled to draw from religious scriptures as sources, just as theologians do, and to draw from phenomenology as a method. I'll draw from anything that will help me clarify the question. And I think by drawing ambidextrously from both, it can open a "middle path" into some interesting questions, even though the Husserlians and the Heideggerians can shout: "Foul! You're bringing religious into this!" and the theologians can say: "Oh, well, you're not a theologian! Did you pass your doctoral exam in dogmatic theology?!" And I just say: "No. I'm just doing a hermeneutic readings of texts — some phenomenological, some religious — and I'm going to mix them. If there be interference, let it be a creative interference. If there be contamination, let it be a fruitful contamination."

MM: In the dialogue Derrida wouldn't provide a theology of the gift, and Marion doesn't. If *you* provided a theology of the gift, what would be some characteristics or axioms?

RK: Well, I repeat, what I'm doing in *The God Who May Be* is not theology as such but a "hermeneutics of religion". It is, I hope, a contribution to the phenomenology of the gift. I usually call "the gift" by other names: (1) the "transfiguring" God; (2) the "desiring" God; (3) the "possibilising" God; (4) the "poeticising" God — the creating God (qua *poesis*). They would be my four categories of gifting. *Poesis* or the poeticising God engages in a co-creation with us. God can't create the kingdom unless we create the space for the kingdom to come.

MM: That's interesting in light of Catherine Keller's thesis that creation *ex nihilo* is too one-way.[7]

RK: What I like about the *creatio ex nihilo* — though I can see that it's non-reciprocal — is that it's an unconditional giving. It's not a giving because there's some problem to be solved that precedes the giving. To use Derrida's language, it comes before economy although it cannot continue without economy. As soon as there's history and finitude and humanity, there's economy, there's negotiation. And there is, to my mind, reciprocity. Here I do disagree with Caputo, Derrida and Lyotard and the postmodern deconstructionists who repudiate the notion of reciprocity or equity or reconciliation. They see it as going back to Hegel or conceding to some kind of economy. I don't think it is as simple as that. I am wary of the polarity between the absolutely-unconditional-gift *versus* the gift-as-compromised-by-the-economy (which gets rid of the gift as pure gift). I just think that's an unhelpful dichotomy, as I think messianicity *versus* messianisms is an unhelpful dichotomy. It's an interesting idea; it's good for an argument. But I think it's ultimately unworkable because I don't think you can investigate messianicity without messianism; and I don't think you can have genuine messianism without messianicity. Now maybe Derrida would agree with that. But there's still a difference of emphasis. I don't see anything wrong with the mix. Whereas Derrida seems to think it is all that is *possible* for us human, mortal beings, but what he's really interested in is the *impossible*. I leave the impossible to God and get on with the possible. Because that's where I find myself: I'm in the economic order. I look to something called "God" — what Derrida calls "the impossible" — to guarantee that the economy doesn't close in on itself. But I don't hold out God as something that we should even entertain as an option for us because God is not an option for us. God is an option for God. Humanity is an option for us. If we can be more human, that's our business. Our business is not to become God. It's God's vocation to become more fully God, ours to become more fully human. We answer to the other without ever *fusing* in some kind of metaphysical unity or identity. When I say "I'm for reciprocity, equity and reconciliation" I'm not for premature Hegelian synthesis. I'm not for metaphysical appropriation or some inevitable evolving "process" of integration. I'm not for reducing the otherness of God to being as such. But, on the other hand, and this may sound paradoxical, I'm all for *traversings* of one by the other — anything that muddies the waters and makes the borders between God and us porous. I don't believe there's an absolute God out there and then a completely compromised humanity here. I think there are constant *to-ings* and *fro-ings*. So the phenomenology of the gift that I'm trying to articulate in terms of poeticizing is a co-creation of history by humanity and God, leading to the kingdom. A new heaven and a new earth. We don't know what that will be because we haven't reached it. We can imagine but we can't pronounce. It goes beyond the sphere of the phenomenology of history because it involves a post-historical situation. It's an *eschaton*. We can imagine it as an eschatology but it's really something that God knows more about than we do.

MM: What do you mean when you say "giving is desiring"?

RK: I argue that giving is desiring because desire is not just the movement from lack to fulfilment, or from potency to act, or from the insufficient to the sufficient — these are metaphysical notions of desire. I'm taking the idea of desire as coming from a fullness towards an absence as much as coming from an absence to a fullness. For example, *kenosis* is a form of desire. And it doesn't come from God being empty and wanting to become full. It comes from God being full and wanting to empty. His divinity in order to be more fully in dialogue with the human because, as Levinas says: "*On s'amuse mieux à deux*". "It's better to be two than one."[8] And it's "better" in the sense of being *more* good, *more* just, *more* loving. It's Eckhart's idea of *ebullutio*, this "bubbling over", this excess or surplus of desire. Not a surplus of being but of desire. Desire is always the desire of more desire. And also the desire for an answer: what's the point in God desiring and having nobody to answer the divine desire? That's why the Song of Songs says it all: the desire of the Shulamite woman — representing humanity — for the Lord or Solomon or the lover, is a desire that actually expresses itself not just as frustration, emptiness, lack, looking for her lover, but as a desire that sings its encounter with the lover that celebrates is *being found*. In the Song of Songs, the lover *finds* the Shulamite woman and that is the inaugural moment, as it were, of the song of desire. It's a desire based not on *fine amor* and romantic passion — which is frustration, prohibition, or absence. It's a desire of plenitude — not of presence, because that's fusional. It's a desire of excess and not of lack. A desire that stems from being taken by God. A response to the desire of the absolute. So that's another form of giving. In other words, the desire of the Shulamite woman is a gift. It's not a subjective hankering. It's a gift; it's a response to a gift. And what's the gift? The gift is desire. So you've got two desires at work. The traditional view has been to consider the human as desiring the fullness of God because the human is full of lack, insufficiency, and finitude. But what I'm trying to do is to see it as much more complex than that. There's a lack in God and there's a lack in humanity. What's the lack in humanity? It's that humanity is not divine. What's the lack in God? God is *not* human. So, in a way, the kingdom as a second coming or incarnation is what we're looking for. But as soon as you have that meeting of the finite and the infinite you've left history behind — not to return to some kind of fusion or "oceanic oneness" *à la* Freud. Let's imagine it hermeneutically, poetically: what would the kingdom be if the desire of the Shulamite woman and the desire of the Lover Lord were to meet and mesh in a post-historical fashion? The first answer is: we don't know. But if we were to imagine it — as various religions have done — it would be a dance; it would be a *perichoresis*. It would be the dance-around of the three persons or of the two lovers and, arguably, where there is two there is always a third. So the *perichoresis* is the refusal — even in *parousia* and *pleroma*, and eschatology and even in the kingdom — to compromise in terms of a closed economy. It never closes. The economy is still bubbling, is still flowering, is still bursting into life and being by virtue of this dance-around which, as *perichoresis*, is something I explore in *The God Who May Be*. The *perichoresis* is the dance-around the *khora*. *Perichora*. The dance-around is each person of the Trinity — whether you interpret that as Father-Son-Holy Ghost, or God-humanity-Kingdom — one doesn't have to be patriarchal and gender-exclusive on this — in dialogue with each other. We're just fanta-

sising here — which of course most theologians wouldn't allow
us to do. They would say: "Well now, is that according to Saint
Thomas or Saint Augustine, etc?" At certain points in history if
you said something like Bruno of Nola or even Eckhart you could
be burnt for it. But let's assume we're not going to be burnt in
this day and age for imagining what might go on in the Kingdom.
Now, in terms of this desiring relationship with the three persons,
there's a double movement that I'm arguing will or *could* continue
— let's imagine — in the kingdom when history has ended as we
know it and when the Shulamite woman who desires God has
come face-to-face with her lover. The double movement is this: it's
a movement of approach and of distance. The term *perichoresis* is
translated into Latin as *circum-in-cessio*, which is taken from *cedo*,
"to leave place", "to absent yourself", and *sedo*, meaning "to sit",
"to assume or take up a position". So there is a double movement
of immanence and transcendence; of distantiation and approxima-
tion. Of moving *towards* each other and then moving *away* from
each other — as in a dance. A dance-around where each other
person cedes their place to the other and then that other to its
other and so on. So it's not just two persons. There's a third person
in this divine dance who you're always acknowledging and invok-
ing. This third person is very important in Levinas and I think it's
very important in certain Christian notions of the Trinity. Because
the danger of two is that two can become one; face-to-face can become a candlelit dinner, where romantic lovers look into each
other's eyes and see themselves reflected in the other. Whereas
the third introduces a little bit of "symbolic castration" that safe-
guards a certain distance and therefore allows for desire. If desire
were to reach its end it would end. And a God who is not desiring
is a God who's not giving. And a God who is not giving is not God.

MM: What about the "transfiguring God"?

RK: The transfiguring God is the God who transfigures us; we
transfigure God. The other example I use is Mount Tabor. Basically, God transfigures us through creation, through interven-
tions in history — whether it's the burning bush or Christ or the
saints or the epiphanies that Joyce and Proust talk about: *that*, to
me, is the divine transfiguring the everyday. So presumably if

God is giving, God is giving as a constant process and practice of transfiguring. We may not see it. We may not know that it's there. And we may refuse to acknowledge it, in which case it doesn't affect our lives. In a way, that's God's loss, too, because if God's transfiguring goes unheeded and unheard, we're going to have wars, evil, and so on. I'm Augustinian in that regard: evil is the *absence* of God as transfiguring, desiring, poeticising, and possibilising — I'll come back to this fourth category in a moment. But transfiguring is not just something God does to us: it's also something that we do to God. And we transfigure God to the extent that we create art, we create justice, we create love. We bring into being, through our actions — poetical and ethical — a transfiguration of the world. It's a human task as much as a divine gift. God gives to us a transfiguring promise; we give back to God a transfigured world — and we can transfigure it in ways that God can't. We can author a poem like a Shakespearean sonnet. God can't do that. But we can co-author with God a poem called *poesis*, creation, the so-called "real" world. That's a different kind of poem, where God and the human meet each other, complement each other. But either can withdraw from the dance, in which case the other just falls on his or her face. That's the end of it. We can destroy God. That's why I speak of a God who *may be*, which is an interpretation of the Hebrew "I am the God who will be, who may be."[9] If I am the God who simply *am*, I am already accomplished, already there, whereas the God who *may be* is *also* a God of promise, of potential, of the kingdom. At any point we can pull the plug on God. As one of the victims of the Holocaust, Etty Hillesum says: "We must help God to be God."[10] And that's where we can make a link with people like Eckhart and Cusanus and some of the other Church Fathers and biblical prophets.

MM: At first glance the notion that "We must help God to be God" sounds arrogant?

RK: Yes, but what it's accepting is that *God is not arrogant*; that God does not presume to be able to stop evil. God can't stop evil. Why? Because evil is the absence of God. God has no power over what God is not — namely evil. God can only be good — unconditionally good in a gifting, loving, creating. That is where the Gnostics and theodicists were wrong: God is not *both* good *and* evil. Even Hegel and Jung made that mistake. God is *not* omnipotent when it comes to evil. God is utterly powerless. And that's terribly important. You find that in the Christian story: Jesus before Pilate, the crucifixion: he couldn't do anything. It's "the power of the powerless" as Vaclav Havel calls it — and he is right. God helps us to be more fully human; we help God to be more fully God — or we don't. If we don't, we can blow up the world and that's the end of humanity, and that's the end of God as the promise of the kingdom because there's nobody there any more to fulfil the promise. In that instance, God remains as pure *desiring*, of course, as pure *poeticising* — except God's world has just been broken up by God's own crea- ture — and God remains *transfiguring*; but there's nothing left to transfigure any more because we've destroyed it.

MM: You also mention the "possibilising God"?

RK: Basically, that means that divinity is a constant offer of the possibility of the Kingdom which can be interpreted in two ways (and you find this in the Scriptures). One is the kingdom as eschatological promise after history, at the *end* of history. The other is the kingdom *now*: in the mustard seed, in the little, everyday, most insignificant of acts. The kingdom is present in the "feast of these". Just as Christ is present in the giving of a cup of cold water. That means that in every moment there is the possibility of good and there is the possibility of non-good. There's the possibility of love; there's the possibility of hate, violence, aggression. We're choosing constantly. And every moment we are actualising the kingdom or not-actualising the kingdom. As Benjamin says so beautifully, "Every moment is a portal through which the Messiah might come." Now what we've got to get away from is thinking that the Messiah comes and then it's all over. If you're a Christian — and I am up to a point: I am a Christian up to the point where the love of "Chris- tians" offends justice and then I'm not "Christian" any more — you draw from the Christian story and testimony the notion that *each little act* makes a difference. For example, the woman with the haemorrhage: you help her — you don't want to but you help her.[11] There's no wine: okay, we reluctantly change the wine.[12] And so on and so forth. You do all of these little things — most of them almost imperceptible — and you don't make a big fuss about it. And when the Messiah comes — even if this happens to be a pretty extraordinary, exemplary instance of the divine in the human — as I believe Christ is — you don't say: "Now it's all over." You *can* say: "Now it's all over for me." But history isn't over. That wasn't the end of the world: the Messiah always comes again in history. And the Messiah is always — including the Christian Messiah — a God who is *still* to come (even when the Messiah has already come). The Messiah is one who has already come and is always still to come. And that's why I see the Christian story as exemplary. (But it's not the only story in town. And, in my view, it has no absolute prerogative vis-à-vis other world religions. God speaks in many voices and in many traditions). But to return to the bible, I could take the Mosaic story as well: in the burning bush God came. With Elijah in the cave the Messiah came. But that wasn't the end of it. The Messiah came in John the Baptist too, the voice crying in the wilderness. It always comes *and* goes. And that's the nature of the Messiah: it's already here — the kingdom is already here — but it is also not yet fully here. And it's that double moment that's terribly important because the possible is not just *the Possible*: the telos of universal history coming to an end at the end of time — that's Hegel. That's triumphalism. That's the kind of monotheistic tyranny that leads to religious wars: "We own The Promised Land"; "*This* and only *this* is the Absolute"; all or nothing. In contrast to such triumphalist teleologies and ideologies of power, the divine possible I am speaking of comes in tiny, almost imperceptible acts of love or in the poetic justice. It's the "music of what happens", as Seamus Heaney says. What Joyce called "epiphanies", Baudelaire "correspondence", Proust "reminiscences". These are testimonies to the possible that becomes incarnate in all these little moments of eschatological enfleshment.

MM: What does "eschatology" mean for you?

RK: If and when the kingdom comes, I believe it will be a great kind of "recollection" or "retrieval" (*anakephalaiosis* is the term used by Paul) of all those special moments of love; but you can't even see it in terms of past, present, and future because the eternal or emblematic is outside time, even though it comes *into* time all the time. Christ is just an exemplary figure of it. What does Christ say at the end? He says: "Time for me to go. Don't touch me. *Noli me tangere.* Don't possess me. I cannot be an idol that you possess." The Messiah is deferred. And here I always draw great sustenance from Blanchot's tale of the beggar waiting for the Messiah at the gates of Rome. The Messiah comes and the beggar goes up to him and says: "Are you the Messiah?" And the Messiah responds: "Yes". And the beggar asks: "When will you come?" because the Messiah is always still to come. The Messiah is there but the Messiah is *still to come* even as the Messiah is *there*. Because we're temporal we're confronted with this unsolvable paradox or aporia — namely that the kingdom has already come and yet is not here. And that's the way it is for our finite phenomenological minds. And no metaphysics and no theology or philosophy can resolve that one. So, to the extent that deconstruction is a reminder of the *impossibility* of ever having the total take on God as absolute, then I'm for deconstruction. But as an endless kind of "soft shoe shuffle" of infinite qualifications and refinements, forever declining any kind of incarnation, I find deconstruction too deserted, too *désertique*, too desert-like, too hard. Derrida's deconstruction is too inconsolable. It's overly uncompromising. Too puritanical — in a way, strangely. It's all about the impossible. But for me, God is the possibilising of the impossible. "What is impossible to us is possible to God."[13] We actualise what God possibilises and God possibilises what remains impossible for us. To sum up: God is giving means God is poeticising, possibilising, transfiguring, and desiring. That's my *religious* phenomenology of the gift. I also did a *pre-religious* phenomenology of the gift in the first part of *Poétique du Possible* publiched in 1984.[14] And if I were to do that again I would certainly include readings of Proust and Joyce or just everyday testimonies to people's kindness, the small ways in which love and creativity works in the world — irrespective of whether people are religious or not. You can go either way.

MM: You've answered the question of a "theology of gift" in terms of thinking *God* as gift. To think *creation* as gift: briefly, what would that entail for you?

RK: If we're talking about divine creation — because I think there's two creations going on: divine and human — I don't want to repeat myself but I would probably go back to the idea of *poesis*: God as *poesis*, the *nous poetikos* as Aristotle calls it, and the *possest* as Cusanus says. Poeticising is the act of constantly opening horizons of possibility, gifts of possibility, for human beings to realise. The divine gift as creation is powerless to impose that gift on somebody who doesn't want it because that would not be good: that would be evil. If you say to somebody, "I love you" and they say, "I don't want your love" and you say, "Sorry, I love you, and whether you like it or not, you are going to be transfigured by my love", that's coercion, violence, tyranny. That's what so-called benevolent dictators do. That's the imposition of the good on somebody who doesn't want it. Sadism in the name of God. How many times has religion done that? The Taliban were doing it. The Inquisition was doing it. The New England Puritans were doing it to the so-called "witches" down in Salem. "For your good, we are going to impose the good!" "But thank you very much, I don't want your good." That's why God loves rebels: God loves the Steven Dedaluses of this world who say: "I will not serve that in which I no longer believe" whether it call itself religion, language or homeland. (It's at the beginning of Joyce's *Portrait of the Artist*.) I suspect that God would prefer people not to serve that in which they do not believe. God prefers honest people who rebel rather than the lackeys, the "creeping Jesuses who would do anything to please us." (Blake) I don't want to get into a cult of the rebel here. But God admires people like Job and David — who argue with God. God admires Jesus on the cross who says: "Why have you forsaken me? Come on, give me an answer to this." God likes that.

MM: In "Desiring God" you mention, quite prophetically: "there is a growing problem of closure to the other. I am sure, if it has not already become a problem here in the United States, it

will become one — the problem of how one can relate openly
and hospitably and justly to the other, without demonisation."[15]
These words obviously resonate in light of the current wave of
terrorism. However, let's ask this question from an ecocentric
perspective: do you have any thoughts on how one can or should
relate openly and hospitably and justly to the non-human other
— animate and inanimate? We demonise the non-human —

RK: We demonise all the time. When people want to show what
the devil is they take an animal. Just look at medieval and Renaissance portraits of demons. The iconography of *The Last Judgment* is full of this, goats, bats, snakes, dragons, griffins, dogs,
gargoyles. I think that's a real question. I think it's something
we in western philosophy and in our excessive anthropo-
centrism have sometimes ignored, that is, the *alterity* of nature:
of trees and of animals, and so on. One thing I've taken great
courage and guidance from is my own children's sensitivity in
this regard. They are vegetarians and very opposed to wearing
fur coats or buying factory-produced food. I think there's a new
and growing awareness in the new generation which is very
important as long as it's kept in balance with being good to
your neighbour who's starving down the street (and perhaps
can only afford factory food). I find there are many young people in Boston or New York who go down to protest against Bush
or the death penalty as much as they will concern themselves
with cruelty to animals and the pollution of nature. The balance
is important. There's no point ignoring social and human issues
out of some kind of obsession with eating "natural" food. That's
just taking food as a surrogate symbol that can be "purified" as
the world disintegrates before the ravages of global poverty
and capitalism. There can sometimes be — for example, the
New England obsession with health and the natural — a demonisation of smoke, a demonisation of alcohol, a demonisation
of sex (although it often goes hand-in-hand with fantasy sex or
sub-world sex in Las Vegas and Hollywood, so it can be very
ambiguous). There is a residual *puritanism* in American culture, I
think, and a certain demonisation of the pagan earthiness of
things. That may include food prohibitions against eating fish or
"killing" tomatoes, etc, as well as the stringent laws against

smoking, drinking, or sexual language. But that's only *half* the story — the *official* version as it were. The other half is very different, and leads to all kinds of perversions and double-think and double-talk. It's a messy world, full of double messages. I'm not saying, therefore, that you should tolerate cruelty to animals and indiscriminately chop down trees. I'm saying you do your best, wherever possible and within the limits of the possible, to remain human while doing the *least* amount of harm to nature or to animals or to your fellow human being. But to pretend that you can enter into some pure realm of pure consumption where everything is as "organic" as in Bread and Circuses food markets is to ignore the fact that Bread and Circuses can only exist for the very wealthy who pay three times as much for their fish and vegetables while the poor have to go to Star Market (a bottom-end supermarket chain) and buy factory-produced food. I approve of going to Bread and Circuses — I just wish it were available to everybody. Somewhere along the line, the refusal of smoke, sex, alcohol, and meat in an *absolutist* fashion can, to my mind, smack of residual puritanism. It can slip into demonisation even with the very best of intentions — and I'm always wary of that. So I would say: "Be vegetarian. Fine. But when you find yourself in a situation where you go to another country and there's only meat on the table, have some meat." If I go to a tribe in Africa and they give me goats' eyeballs, I may not particularly like it, but I'm not going to offend my host by saying: "I don't eat goats' eyeballs!" I'll eat it — raw or cooked. That's the kind thing to do. That's accepting the hospitality of the other as other. Or as the Dalia Lama advised his monks, "eat whatever is dropped into your begging bowl".

MM: In *The God Who May Be* you open up the question of discernment, whether we're facing saturation or the desert. You claim that: "For the theist Marion, no less than for the atheist Derrida, we are left with the dilemma of 'holy madness', how to judge between true and false prophets, between good and evil ghosts, between holy and unholy messiahs."[16] Even though Caputo and Derrida are suspicious of criteria — I guess we all are a little suspicious — how should we nevertheless judge between the true and the false, the good and the evil? After Derrida, how do you treat criteria?

RK: You do so by trying to discern and judge more carefully, more cautiously, more critically. And I would say more hermeneutically. You don't have to get rid of criteria altogether. Derrida would say: "Well, of course we have to make decisions all the time. We judge and we use criteria. We have to do that: we couldn't not do it." Strictly speaking, that's already a compromise. That's already entering into the economy of things. And I just find the gap between our decisions and undecidability too polar. That's my problem: it's too antithetical, too aporetical, too impossible. Decisions are "too difficult" in the deconstructive scenario. They're all made in "fear and trembling" because we're "in the dark"! At the 1999 Villanova exchange I asked Derrida: "How can you read in the dark?" He said: "We can *only* read in the dark." But I want to turn the light on! Even if it's only a flashlight — that will remove a little of the darkness and confusion. I don't believe in *absolute* light or total enlightenment for us ordinary mortals. It doesn't have to be either absolute light or total darkness. It doesn't have to be that hard. We're not all desperate Desert Fathers waiting for Godot as the apocalyptic dusk descends! It doesn't have to be that angst-ridden or melodramatic. The world's a place of light and dark: we always have a bit of both.

MM: Derrida might say that the world is in such a mess because we assume we can read in the light and that all decisions are easy.

RK: I can understand what he's saying in the light of an excessive *hubris* and arrogance on behalf of the Enlightenment, on behalf of rationalism, on behalf of science and technology. There I agree with him. But I'm not sure that's the way most people in the world today actually think or live. Most people are confused and bewildered. They're not cock-sure *cogitos* in need of deconstruction but wounded, insecure, fragile subjects in search of meaning.

MM: What about religious dogmatism?

RK: Oh, before the Enlightenment it was worse. What I'm saying is: to think you possess the light and everybody else is in
darkness is a recipe for imperialism, colonisation, injustice,
holy war, *jihad*, "Good versus Evil." We're witnessing it again
today. Nobody has a prerogative on light or the good. That
doesn't mean we're all condemned to a kind of total darkness,
khora, undecidability. I think everything should be decon-
structed, but the question for me is: what's it like *after* deconstruction? That's why I still believe in hermeneutics. Derrida
doesn't. I believe in reminiscences, resurrections, reconciliations. They're all temporary, they're all provisional, they're all
muddling through. Granted — but they do happen. I believe in
paths. Not massive metaphysical viaducts or Golden Gate
Bridges between the contingent and the absolute, but I do believe in little footbridges — the kind you get in Harrison Ford
movies. Hermeneutic bridges, connections, ladders. I find that
deconstruction follows the template of the Lazarus parable: the
implacable metaphor of the gulf that a) separates paradise, the
Absolute, the impossible from b) the land of the living — our
finite, everyday, contingent, mortal world. The deconstructive
gulf radically segregates the two. There's an unbridgeable gap
between the divine and the human, the impossible and the possible. The deconstructionist Abraham won't allow Lazarus to
send a message back to his brothers to warn and instruct them.
It is too late. The kind of hermeneutics of religion that I'm talking about, by contrast, would be more guided by the paradigm
of Jacob's ladder, where there's *to-ing* and *fro-ing*, lots of people going up and down, in both directions. No *absolute* descent
or *absolute* ascent. It's little people going up and down ladders.
And that, to me, is how you work towards the kingdom. "Every
step you take . . ." (as the song goes). Each step counts. Messianic incursion, incarnation, epiphany is a possibility for every
moment of our lives. But because we are finite and temporal,
the infinite can pass through time, but it can never remain or
take up residence in some absolute or permanent present.
That's the difference between the eternal and time. They can
criss-cross back and forth, up and down, like the angels on

Jacob's ladder. But they are never identical, never the same. That's what a hermeneutic affirmation of *difference* is all about. As opposed to deconstructive *différance* which in my view, gives up hope in the *real possibility* of mediation and transition.

MM: One more question generated by "Desiring God". Whereas someone like Marion may turn to mystical theology and a phenomenology of saturation, I concur with you in your affirmation of "hermeneutical retrievals and re-imaginings of biblical narratives and stories."[17] Could you briefly comment on the possible nature or direction of these retrievals and re-imaginings? And could you perhaps suggest how such retrievals could inform — and be informed by — a philosophical theology of gift/ing? For Kevin Hart and Jean-Luc Marion and others, they draw from mystical theology, but they seem to be turning away from biblical resources.

RK: That's why I'm into the hermeneutics of narrative imagination, whereas they're into a deconstructionist position (yes, even Marion in my view) — and there *is* a difference in that regard. So while I learn from deconstruction, I really am closer to hermeneutics — I try to negotiate between the two, but I'm closer to hermeneutics — what I call a "diacritical hermeneutics". It's not the romantic hermeneutics of Gadamer and Heidegger and Schleiermacher: getting back to the original event and re-appropriating the inaugural moment. I don't believe in that kind of biblical hermeneutics as a retrieval of the original and the originary — some primal unity. Nor would I uncritically endorse what Jack Caputo calls "radical hermeneutics" — which is really another word for deconstruction — because it doesn't really allow, in my view, for valid retrievals, recognitions or reconciliations. In *Strangers, Gods and Monsters* I propose a diacritical hermeneutics which is a third way.[18] I propose mediations, connections, inter-links and passages back and forth. So it's neither re-appropriation and fusion of horizons à *la* Gadamer, nor is it a complete gulf, separation, or rupture à *la* Caputo, Lyotard, and Derrida. Diacritical hermeneutics holds that faith is helped by narratives. Now I don't privilege in any exclusivist sense the Christian narratives over the Jewish or the Islamic or the non-monotheistic. I just say: "They're the ones I know best." If I was a Muslim, I'd work with Muslim narratives. If I was Jewish, I'd work with Jewish texts. (Indeed, as a Christian, I generally work with both Christian *and* Jewish narratives.) My niece has become a Buddhist: I learn from Buddhist stories and I try to include them in my work. I still do it from a Christian perspective because that's what I'm most familiar with. But if I'd grown up in Kyoto, I would invoke the Buddhist texts first. I don't believe that any religion has an absolute right to the Absolute. There is no one, Royal Route. There should be no proprietal prerogatives here. They're all narrative paths towards the Absolute. And if you happen to be born on this particular road or highway rather than another one, and you've walked it for twenty or thirty years, then you know it better than another one, and you can help other people walk it. And from your knowledge of it, when you come to a crossroads, you may have more interesting and intelligent dialogue with the person who has come along the other highway. You know where you've come from and you can talk to them about it. And they can learn from you and you can learn from them. Whereas if you say immediately: "Oh well, to hell with my highway! I'm really more interested in yours" they can say: "Well, I'll tell you about mine, but do you have anything to add to the conversation?" And you'll say: "No, no! I hate everything about my road! I've learnt nothing. That's only a load of baloney!" I'm always a bit suspicious of zealous converts who repudiate everything in their own traditions and look to some New Age trendy alternative for a solution — and that can be a Buddhist becoming a Christian as much as a Christian becoming a Buddhist. I'm all for dialogue between the two. Some people have to change their religions to shake off the tyranny of their tradition. Their experience may be *so* negative that they *need* to do that. And here you can have a kind of religious or cultural transvestism that is very helpful: you wear the clothes of another religion and through it you can see the spiritual in a way which you couldn't have done previously. I'm not against conversion as such unless it's from an absolutist disposition to another absolutist disposition. I don't think any religion should be absolutist. I think it should be searching for the Absolute but the *search itself* should not be absolutist because that's to presume we preserve the Absolute. Where I am wary of a certain mystical New Ageism or deconstructionism is their tendency to repudiate historical narratives and memories as invariably compromising and totalising. I see narratives and memories as necessary mediations. If you don't go down the route of hermeneutic re-interpretation — which is a long route, as Ricoeur says, an arduous labor of reading and rereading. Then you must go towards the desert like Derrida and Caputo and their ana-khorites. Which is hard. Or else you go towards the opposite, mystical extreme — not towards *khora* this time but towards the "saturated phenomenon" or hyperessential divinity (with Marion or Michel Henri). But then it's another kind of "holy terror" because you're completely *blinded* by it. You embrace another kind of "dark" (from over-exposure to the Absolute in the dark night of the soul). Here too, it seems to me, there's no interpretation possible. It's immediate, non-mediated presence. In both cases — whether you're going into the emptiness and undecidability of the *khora* or whether you're going into the blinding over-exposed splendor of God — you are subjected to an experience of "holy madness". Now, I'm not against that *as a moment*. But you can't live with the moment: you've got to interpret it after the event. Otherwise, what's the difference between Moses and the burning bush and Peter Sutcliffe in his lorry claiming he's illuminated and hearing a so-called divine voice that says: "Go and kill prostitutes and do my will and clear the world of this evil scourge"?[19] What's the difference? There *must* be a difference. And we must try to discern as best we can between (a) psychopaths like Charlie Manson, Peter Sutcliffe, or Jack the Ripper, who think they're on a *divine* mission to kill in the name of God, and (b) prophets like Moses or Isaiah, who go out to liberate and comfort their enslaved people. You have to be able to *even vaguely* and approximately tell the difference. No?

MM: So we return to the problem of Abraham sacrificing his son?

RK: Yes, but my reading of this episode is very different to Kierkegaard's and closer to Levinas's. The way to read that, I suggest, involves a critical hermeneutic retrieval. The story illustrates how monotheistic revelation is anti-sacrifice; it marks a move away from human sacrifice. This may be read therefore as a story about the transition from a pre-monotheistic or pre-revelation stage to revelation. The first voice that Abraham hears — "Kill your son" — is, by this account, his *own voice*. It's the voice of his ancestral, tribal sacrificial religion. But the second voice that says "Do *not* kill your son" is the voice of the kingdom. That's how I read it. I think we should read every story in the Gospel according to the principle: "where is justice being preached here and where is injustice?" Where there's evil, you have to say no to it. You can find other passages in the Bible that say: "Go out and kill all Gentiles or Canaanites." If you take that literally you're into the Palestinian/Israeli situation. You are into Holy War. Ditto for the Christian invocation of a "blood libel" against Jews. We should read such texts hermeneutically, critically, and say: "No! That was an interpolation by certain zealous Zionist scribes during a certain century . . ." We need historical research on this. We need to demythologise it and say: They were trying to justify the occupation of their neighbors' lands. So ignore that mispresentation of divine revelation and look rather to the Psalm where God calls for the protection of the widow, the stranger, and the orphan. The stranger is your neighbor — *that's* God speaking. "Go out and kill Canaanites" is *not* God speaking — that's *us* speaking. Knowing the difference is a matter of hermeneutic discernment. And it's a matter which concerns every believer, every reader of Scripture.

MM: Nietzsche asks, "Can there be a God beyond good and evil?"[20] Maybe we're just projecting our idea that God is "simply good"; that God can only do "purely good things"?

RK: Everyone makes their choice, but the God of love and justice is the only God I'm interested in. I'm not interested in the God of evil, torture and sadism. I'm just not interested in that Gnostic (or neo-Gnostic) notions that see the dark side of God — destruction and holocaust — as an indispensable counterpart to the good side. Such theories or theodicies can justify *anything*.

MM: But there is that possibility?

RK: There *isn't* that possibility — not for me. It's how you interpret it. You can, of course, interpret divinity in terms of a moralising God where you say: "Oh, homosexuality, masturbation,
sex outside of marriage, etc is evil." That's the Christian Coali-
tion, Pat Buchanan, Ian Paisley — they seem to know what's
good for all of us! I'm against such a *moralising* God but I'm not
against an *ethical* God. There's a big difference. I *don't know*
what the absolutely good is. How could anyone know? But I do
believe — precisely because I can't know — and I will do everything to try to differentiate and discern (according to what
Ignatius calls "the discernment of spirits") as best I can between the God of love and the pseudo-god of hate. I do believe
that the divine is the good. In fact "God" is another name for
"the good" rather than "the good" being another name for
God. We don't know what the good is. We don't know what
God is either. But they *must* be the same because if they're,
there's no way to avoid theodicy: "This war was necessary. It's
all part of the will of God. It's the necessary dark side to God."
Jung's answer to Job. Pangloss's answer to the Lisbon earth-
quake. Hegel's answer to the Terror. The rise of Divine Reason
run amok. As humans, I agree, we have to confront the *thanatos*,
the shadow in ourselves, the sadistic instincts, the perversions,
the hate, the evil, the aggression. *We* have to confront the
shadow in ourselves. But divinity doesn't have to confront the
shadow in itself — because if it has evil in itself it is not God. If
you say "The shadow in God — the sacrifice of innocent children, torture of victims — is part of God's will" well, I'd prefer
to burn in hell than believe in a God who justifies the torture of
innocent children. And I'm not ambiguous about that. That said,
I take a very dramatic example here that very few people
would say is good because on many occasions it's very hard to
tell what's absolutely good or evil. But it is very hard for people
to justify the torture of an innocent child. Should the Americans
have dropped the atomic bomb in Hiroshima? I would say
"No," but I'm not going to be too moralistic about that because I
know there's an argument. You can negotiate that. Should a
woman have an abortion? I would say: "Ideally not, but it's her

right, and she's doing what she thinks is right, and, on balance, it may be the right thing for her to do." So I think a law that says "You can never have an abortion" is wrong. Abortion is very complex. It can be right in some respects, and wrong in others — *at the same time*. And it's right and it's wrong. Morality is grey on grey; it's not black and white. Let's just say it is morally difficult. And everyone — for or against — has a right to discuss it. That's what morality is. It's not about absolutes. But when it comes to God, who is absolute, either God is good or I'm not interested in God. This mixing evil with God is gnosticism. I wrote my second novel, *Walking at Sea Level*, as an argument against that.

MM: There are all these other metaphysical characteristics ascribed to God: God is one, God is pure, and so on, and to say, "God is purely good" —

RK: Well, I'm not sure I would use the word "purely" here because then you're back into puritanism. But I do insist on the claim that God is unconditionally and absolutely good or God is not God. I would not claim that I know what the good is. I would simply *try* to discern better what is good and what is evil or what is better and what is worse, what is more or less just in a *given* situation. I can recognize many instances of good acts where people put others before themselves and give up their life or gives up their wealth — that, to me, is a good thing to do. I want to reserve the right to say that. Whereas when somebody chops a child's head off, I want to be able to say: "That's *not* a good thing." I think most people would agree. That's not an absolutist disposition: it is common sense, practical wisdom, what the Greeks called *phronesis*, the Latins *prudential*. Whenever someone does a good act — gives a cup of cold water to a parched neighbor — he or she is making God that little bit *more* real and actual and incarnate in the world. When someone does evil — torturing innocent children or simply stealing the cup of cold water from the parched neighbor who needs it more — he or she is refusing the possibilising, desiring, transfiguring promise of God. In that sense evil is the refusal to let God exist.

MM: In your legendary 1984 interview with Derrida, he explains that there have always been "heterogeneous elements" in Christianity.[21] Was he referring to scriptural motifs or mystical theology? Or both?

RK: I don't know. You'd have to ask him. But I suspect that what he means by that is probably similar to what I've just been saying: there's no one pure religion. Christianity is heterogeneous. It draws from pagan elements, Jewish elements, Greek elements, etc.

MM: The context was Greek philosophy or metaphysics, mainstream Christianity, and you referred to the official dogmas of the dominant churches, and then Derrida said: "Oh, no, I can see that there are heterogeneous elements." But I didn't know if he meant biblical theology and some of the mystical texts.

RK: Generally speaking, when Derrida says, "There are heterogeneous elements" that's good news from his point of view. So I think he just wants to say: "Look, as I would interpret it, Christianity isn't just this triumphalist, totalising, dogmatic, absolutist, intolerant body of beliefs. It's actually quite porous and permeable to dialogue with its other." And I would agree with him wholeheartedly here.

MM: And there are marginal voices there.

RK: Exactly.

MM: Having cited that line, do you think Derrida prefers the biblical over the mystical?

RK: It depends how you define "the biblical" and "the mystical." There are elements of the mystical in Derrida. He is very taken, for example, by Pseudo-Dionysius, Eckhart, Silesius, Cusanus. But I think there are other forms of mysticism that Derrida would not have much time for: particularly the fusional and somewhat hysterical claim to be "one with God".

MM: I haven't read many mystical theologians, but most of them say we can't speak about God and then —

RK: They go on and speak about God.

MM: And affirm all the dogmas and say "God is definitely Trinitarian," "God is this" and "God is that" and they just seem to slide back into this totalising discourse.

RK: Then they're not really good mystics, I would say.

MM: Wouldn't mystical theology — taken to its logical or a/logical conclusion — have to say: "So I'm going to suspend my beliefs on, say, the creeds of the churches, because the creeds are as positive as you can get." I was just wondering how the mystics balanced their mysticism with their denominational affirmations. Dionysius wasn't considered a heretic.

RK: Most of them were. Eckhart was. John Scotus Eriugena was. Bruno and Vico were. They were in favor one moment, out the next. These thinkers were trying to make sense to their fellow believers. They had had these deep, spiritual experiences and were profoundly touched and were trying to reconcile these experiences with the doctrine of the Virgin Birth or the Filioque or something like that. They were mucking along. They were trying to be loved and accepted by their brethren in the monastery. Otherwise they were out in the rain with no food. We compromise and we muddle through. I would say here, again, that Derrida often discriminates: he picks and chooses — and rightly so. He's an *à la carte* rabbinical interpreter. Just think of his reflections on biblical passages in *Schibboleth* or "Circumfession", for example.[22] Or again in *Donner la mort* (*The Gift of Death*) where Derrida goes back to the Abraham story.[23] He takes what inspires him and rejects the kind of Zionist triumphalism which says: "Death to all Arabs." So he discriminates. You might say: ""Well, *how* do you discriminate, Mr. Derrida, since there are no criteria and we can only read in the dark?" But that's another day's work. Maybe it's a performative contradiction but, happily, he does exercise it. He discriminates.

He differentiates. He discerns. He's on the side of the good. Deconstruction is not a justification for genocide and holocaust. It's not an apologia for an "anything goes" relativism — as some of its critics suggest.

MM: In the end, deconstruction is just trying to affirm that whatever is going in the world —

RK: No, that's Heidegger. Derrida's saying: "I'm for justice. I'm for the gift. I'm for the good. I'm for the democracy to come." He's not saying: "It doesn't matter whether it's democracy or totalitarianism. It doesn't matter whether it's justice or injustice. It doesn't matter whether it's gift or selfishness." He's not saying that at all. Derrida is on the side of the good. All his thinking, politically and ethically, is emancipatory. The differences I have with Derrida are not in terms of his values, his ethics, his politics — but how one gets there. That's a practical question, a pragmatic question. I think hermeneutics, *informed by* a certain deconstructive caution, vigilance and scrupulosity, is a better way of getting there than deconstruction on its own (without hermeneutics). That's where I part company with Caputo, Derrida and Lyotard. But they're all on the side of the good as I see it. I'm not saying: "We're all morally pure." I'm saying that the good is something we aspire to, something that is impossible, something that is "impossible" in its *absolute* sense but possible in all kinds of different tiny practical ways. The messianic is potentially present in every moment, even though we can never be sure whether it comes or goes.

Notes

---

[1] "On the Gift: A Discussion between Jacques Derrida and Jean-Luc Marion, Moderated by Richard Kearney" in *God, the Gift, and Postmodernism*, ed. John D. Caputo and Michael J. Scanlon (Bloomington/Indianapolis: Indiana University Press, 1999) pp. 54-78, 61.

[2] Geoffrey Bennington and Jacques Derrida, *Jacques Derrida*, trans. Geoffrey Bennington (Chicago: University of Chicago Press, 1993) p. 154.

[3] Jean-Luc Marion, *God Without Being*, trans. Thomas A. Carlson (Chicago: The University of Chicago Press, 1991).

[4] Jean-Luc Marion, "Le phénomène saturé" in *Phénoménologie et théologie*, ed. Jean-François Courtine (Paris: Criterion, 1992) pp. 79-128. "The Saturated Phenomenon," trans. Thomas A. Carlson, *Philosophy Today* 40 (1996), pp. 103-124. See also *Phenomenology and the "Theological Turn"*, Dominique Janicaud *et al* (New York: Fordham University Press, 2000).

[5] Martin Heidegger, *Introduction to Metaphysics*, trans. Gregory Fried and Richard Polt (New Haven: Yale University Press, 2000)

[6] Richard Kearney, *The God Who May Be: A Hermeneutics of Religion* (Bloomington: Indiana University Press, 2001).

[7] See Catherine Keller's *The Face of the Deep: A Theology of Becoming* (London: Routledge, 2002).

[8] Emmanuel Levinas, "Ethics of the Infinite" in Richard Kearney, *States of Mind: Dialogues with Contemporary Thinkers* (New York: New York University Press, 1995) pp. 177-199.

[9] Exodus 3.14.

[10] Etty Hillesum, *An Interrupted Life* (New York: Owl Books, 1991). Cited in *The God Who May Be*.

[11] Mt 9.19-23; Lk 8.43-48.

[12] Jn 2.1-11.

[13] Mt 10.27, 19.26; Lk 18.27.

[14] Richard Kearney, *Poétique du Possible: Phénoménologie Herméneutique de la Figuration* (Paris: Beauchesne, Paris, 1984).

[15] "Desire of God" (with Discussion) in *God, the Gift, and Postmodernism*, edited by John D. Caputo and Michael J. Scanlon (Bloomington/Indianapolis: Indiana University Press, 1999) pp. 112-145, 135.

[16] "Desire of God", note 43, p. 140.

[17] "Desire of God", note 43, p. 139.

[18] Richard Kearney, *Strangers, Gods and Monsters* (London/New York: Routledge, 2002).

[19] Peter Sutcliffe is the serial killer known as the "Yorkshire Ripper". He claimed that his killing spree was a divine mission.

[20] Nietzsche asks in Section 55 of the *Will to Power* (ed. Walter Kaufmann, trans. Walter Kaufmann and R. J. Hollingdale, New York: Vintage Books, 1968): "Does it make sense to conceive a god 'beyond good and evil'?"

[21] Richard Kearney asks Derrida the following question in his interview with him in *Dialogues with Contemporary Continental Thinkers: the Phenomenological Heritage: Paul Ricoeur, Emmanuel Levinas, Herbert Marcuse, Stanislas Breton, Jacques Derrida* (Manchester: Manchester University Press, 1984): "But did not Judaism and Christianity represent a heterogeneity, an 'otherness' before they were assimilated into Greek culture?" To which Derrida replied: "Of course. And one can argue that these original, heterogeneous elements of Judaism and Christianity were never completely eradicated by Western metaphysics. They perdure throughout the centuries, threatening and unsettling the assured 'identities' of Western philosophy. . . ." pp. 116-117.

[22] Jacques Derrida's *Schibboleth — pour Paul Celan* (Paris: Galilée, 1986) and "Circumfession: Fifty-nine Periods and Periphrases" form the text *Jacques Derrida*, co-written ("Derridabase") and trans. Geoffrey Bennington (Chicago: University of Chicago Press, 1993).

[23] Derrida's essay "Donner la mort" appears in the book *L'Ethique du don: Jacques Derrida et la pensée du don*, eds. Jean-Michel Rabaté and Michael Wetzel (Paris: Métailié-Transition, 1992). The English version of the essay is titled *The Gift of Death*, trans. David Wills (Chicago: University of Chicago Press, 1995).

Chapter 7

A SEARCH AND SOME FINDINGS

Cathy Molloy

I think it's better to be honest from the outset. So, I'm owning up at the start, pleading guilty right away. I love the Church! Middle age has taught me to accept several of the mysteries of life. Like, for instance, that belief and unbelief, curiosity and apathy, anger and affection, outrage and pride, and delight and abhorrence can be contained within an overall love for this Roman Catholic Church which is such a big part of my life.

THE CHURCH THEN

From as far back as I can recall I had quite a few problems in the faith department. I never did believe the Adam and Eve and the forbidden fruit story. I knew the story well. I loved the story. But a God who would create people with a questioning mind and then punish them for wanting to know never made sense to me. It still doesn't.

Then there was the question of church and going to Mass, which I loved. The idea of "God's house" held a great fascination for me. The sounds of the ceremony, prayers chanted or muttered, familiar and strange at once, bell ringing, the distribution of the wafers of bread that was more than bread, the people gathered together in this action of worship of, and sharing in the God who made us all, and who would be pleased by it all, always made sense to me. It still does.

Then there was Jesus and the crib and God loving us, and wanting to be with us, which made great sense, and then the awful shock of the cross and us not loving God, and wanting to be rid of him in such a violent way, which made no sense at all. God had sent his precious, only son (which was so much more significant, apparently, than if he had sent a daughter) and this had been the result. If only he had kept his precious son and sent us down one of the girls things might have been a whole lot different. At least it seemed that people would not have been so scandalously guilty if they had crucified one of the girls. What was it about boys and girls that accounted for the difference in regard? God had made us all hadn't he?

Later, a more knowing look, and the things that made sense still made sense, and the things that made no sense still made no sense. And still there was the issue of why there were no girls to be seen serving at the altar — a job I envied so much with its red and white flowing outfit and the bell-ringing and what not; and why I was invisible, standing beside my brother, when the priest asked my mother if the boys would like to be altar servers, a scenario that would be repeated some twenty five years later for the benefit of my own daughter. But by this time I had eaten a little of that fruit that Eve had tasted in the garden and was risking the wrath of God in wanting some knowledge of what might be good and what not so.

Soon I would have so many questions that would disturb me greatly. If God made and loves us all how come there are rich and starving people? How come there are sick and well people? How come there are countries where most people have enough, and to spare, and other countries where no one, it seems, has enough, and most are dying from lack of the basic necessities of life? If God made and loves us all how come some of those he loves love others greatly in return, and others think little of hurting, even to destroying others in return?

Why *is* there something rather than nothing? Who are we? What are we like? What are we for? As Boyle asks, in O'Casey's *Juno and the Paycock*, "What *is* the stars?" In my experience most children have asked the basic philosophical questions by the time they are four or five years old. Most children quickly let go of them since most adults, if they respond at all, give answers which are by definition unsatisfactory. The questions may or may not emerge to be articulated in the adolescent years, but it seems to me that our culture makes it difficult for people, perhaps especially young people, who are concerned by other concerns than the immediate, to pursue their questions or wonderings in any meaningful way. Ours is an age of frenetic movement; multiple media competing for our attention on a daily if not hourly basis; we so easily make the mistake of believing that what is most important is what others decide should be the headlines. Timetables are full, even what might be considered leisure pursuits, for adults or children, can often be fraught by pressures of getting there, performance, competition and so on. The pressure to achieve according to a narrow set of criteria dominates so much of life for many people. Eventually for me, the issue became whether to spend precious disposable time practising a sport, or to pursue the questions that had fascinated me from early childhood. The wondering won out.

A Search and Some Findings

It was not until the early 1980s that I had the opportunity to do something concrete in this regard, and my search began in earnest. Returning to Ireland after a period away, and becoming increasingly frustrated at the debates about the contraception and divorce issues, as a card-carrying and Mass-going Catholic I needed to know not just what the teachers and preachers of my church were saying about them, but why they said it. What were they teaching the teachers and preachers? How had we come to where we were then? There were things I wanted to know. A course in moral theology seemed the thing to pursue. And so the search into some of the "whys" began in a formal and organised way. But you don't begin with a course in moral theology, I soon found out. It involved beginning at the beginning with two years of philosophy followed by three of theology at the Milltown Institute of Philosophy and Theology in Dublin.

In philosophy the great sweep of the history of thinking was fascinating to me, but it was the courses based mainly on the work of Bernard Lonergan, the Canadian Jesuit, philosopher and theologian, that I found most immediately satisfying.[1] The

meaning of thought, knowledge and action was opened out in a
new way for me. Along with the perennial questions, the questions of our time were of necessity included in tracing the line
from the sense experience of the individual to the possibility of
what would be described as mystical knowing. What is happening when we know? When we know that we know? Lonergan's
concept of the human person as "the pure desire to know"
made great sense to me.

Questioning is our nature, beginning with the need to understand our immediate surroundings and situation. Being unsatisfied until the questions are answered to the point of the "virtually
unconditioned", which in turn leads us to the next question, is a
manifestation of "the pure desire to know". The inbuilt pattern of
reflection on experience — beginning with sense experience,
leading to understanding and then to a judgement on the truth or
falsehood of our understanding, and a judgement of value —
must issue in action if we are being true to our desire for authen-
ticity. Wanting to know the truth of things, that it matters whether
something is really good or just seems to be so, is not just the
territory of the sceptic but the point of human questioning. To
understand that taking a look is not knowing, that our desire for
truth and integrity will leave us unsatisfied if we take short cuts
with our basic desire to know, and to act in line with our knowing, resonated strongly with my own experience. The idea that it
is possible to know and choose the good, that objectivity is possible with authentic subjectivity, that being faithful to the pattern
of understanding and judgements can lead beyond immediate
satisfaction to the pursuit of value, gives me cause for hope.
Awareness of individual and collective bias, openness to being
changed, and conversion, intellectual, moral and ultimately even
religious, is central to this way of seeing things, and to the attempt to live authentically out of it. Although I related to this primarily at the individual level it is equally true that groups and
indeed societies struggle to be true to their self-understanding.
The pull in opposing directions, "that which I will, I do not, and
that which I will not, I do" that St Paul describes, is present in
many levels of human action.

The capacity for self-transcendence, that we can move beyond self-interest and choose what is really good over what

seems to be so, gives hope and a sense of point to every human effort for a better world. Every effort for improvement matters, even those that may seem like a waste of time, a drop in the ocean. What we do about plastic bags or unwanted kittens is more closely connected to the basic questions than might be immediately obvious.

Of course the other side of this is that often we do not act in line with our knowing, we choose against what we know to be the good, and here experience dis-ease, and disquiet and discomfort, anxiety and guilt and shame, and we have our ways of dealing with that, resulting in blocks to human flourishing of minor and major proportions. This too resonated with my own experience. Considered in relation to how societies operate, our own being the obvious example, then I find it logical to relate some of the more obvious ills of our society to the fact that, as a group, we seem to be unwilling or unable to consider the good of all when making some fundamental choices. The resulting unjust structures and systems, housing, health and education for example, may not be entirely responsible for all that goes wrong, but most certainly block the possibility of well-being for very many people. It seems to me that to be human is to be on the spectrum, from petty one-upmanship — like cutting across others in conversation, or not giving way in the traffic — through bullying and exploitation, to gross misuse of power in individual and group situations, right to the point of the killing and destruction of wars on the one hand. And equally we are capable of operating on the other side, by the smallest actions for something or someone other than self, right through boundless generosity to the ultimate, the free giving up of life itself for someone or something on whom or on which we place the maximum value.

THE GOD QUESTION

But where does the God question come into it? I believe the question of God is implicit in all our questioning. Even if all the goods of health, education, security, and wealth were in our possession, still we would want to know who we are and what we are for. We are reasonable people, and so faith, while by definition not justified by any certainty in the accepted sense of the word, cannot fly totally in the face of our experience. The un-caused cause, the design argument, the ontological argument of Anselm — "that being than which nothing greater can be con-ceived" — have their merits and flaws as reasons for believing or not in God. The desire to know, expressed in human question-ing, as I understand it, can only have what I understand to be God as its answer. To me, it is reasonable to infer from this de-sire to know that there is some intelligent source of this desire, some intelligent, meaningful term (end/goal) for it. Attentiveness to the data of consciousness, and the ever-present need for con-version at many levels, is essential in the ongoing attempt to make sense of life, and put pieces together in the reaching to-wards what is truer, what I hope and believe is good, what draws me by its beauty. To know that I share the desires and the search with countless seekers of other great world religions and of none is humbling and exhilarating at the same time.

But of course no one has ever seen God. For me, glimpses of truth, goodness or beauty, fleeting apprehensions of love and self-giving, in this or that relationship, or encounter, or situa-tion, or location, continue to be enough to hold my faith in the Being whose being and essence I understand to be the perfec-tion, or completion, or fullness of these. Maybe it does not go without saying that having also to face the nothing, to contem-plate the absence of meaning, to be for a time in no place, to taste the edges, if not the depths, of despair, can lead to an ap-preciation of the fact that, however reasonable I find faith to be, it is none the less a gift. I am content to be in the company of those who, like Augustine, seek not to understand so that I may believe, but rather believe in order that I may understand.

THEOLOGY

Faith, like many gifts, can be a burden too. But, gift or burden or both, it is not exempt from the questions. We humans are mainly reasonable people. Why believe in the God of the Old and New Testaments? What about Abraham and the need to be willing to trust so completely in God, even in the face of outra-geous demands by any human standard? Who was the Jesus person? What was he about? He came, we learn in the Gospel of John, "that we might have life, and have it to the full". His life and work and teaching, as we have it in the Gospels, tell us about who we are, and what we are for, who God is for us, and who we can be for one another and for God. From the many ways he tried to teach and show this, countless people down the generations have found it good news that we are not simply the "ghost in the machine", that we are more than we appear at first. It is good news that the "godness" that is through us, and which we so effectively block with our many and varied schemes and detours, will not be entirely quenched. It is good news that not only may we hope to make this a better world but that we are made for it despite the blocks and detours. It is good news that despite the awfulness of much human experience, love is greater still, and we can have hope in some fulfilment of our being, as the Christian understanding of resurrection promises.

But Christian theology teaches that this fulfilment begins here, in this world in which we live now, it is now, although not yet complete. We each have our part to play in responding positively to instances of the beginning, which is announced by Jesus in the new Testament, for ourselves and for those with whom we share our time on earth. We have responsibility too, to those who will come after us, and whose wellbeing will depend, to an extent at least, on the decisions we make about what would be good for ourselves, for others, and for the earth and its resources. It seems to me reasonable to believe in a God and a creation in whom and in which we live and move and have our being, and with whom and with which we are co-creators and co-operators, in so far as our choices and actions tend towards human wellbeing in its fullest sense. A fundamental point is that this does not mean that the meaning of ultimate wellbeing or "heaven" is in our gift, or dependent entirely on what we do. Rather it is to say that it begins here and now, and it is in our God-given humanness to live our lives in such a way that it increases with our efforts in the spirit of Christ, and in that spirit we have hope for its completion in the One we call God.

Liberation theology, theology in which Scripture is understood as a narrative of liberation, is an expression for our time of the words and work of Jesus who came "to bring good news to the poor", who came so "that we might have life to the full". Some of its characteristics are orientation towards the poor and oppressed, emphasis on praxis in the light of Scripture, and its understanding of the nature of salvation as the completion of liberation.[2] Beginning from the context of oppression of large sections of the population in South America its method has been shown to be applicable in many other situations too. Within Christianity, oppression and injustice in relation to gender, race, sexual orientation, and social class have been addressed, resulting in varying degrees of raised awareness and change by the method of liberation theology. Recognition of the inter-dependence of people and peoples, engagement with justice issues, work for justice, are shown to be at the core of what it means to be Christian and specifically to be Catholic. Salvation is not all about some other existence, but begins now. That there is this connection between human liberation and salvation means that, where human potential and wellbeing is limited or prevented for many people by unjust systems or structures, do-ing nothing is not an option. Sin is not just a matter of my actions as an individual, but is present also in many structures and sys-tems. This, of course, applies very obviously to the systems and structures within the church itself. Liberation theology is a way of doing theology that begins with the experience of oppres-sion, and, in the light of the gospel, sets out to uncover and change the unjust structures and systems that are at its root, to unmask ideologies that conceal what is happening in concrete human reality.[3] Belief in a God who is love and whose presence in our world is where compassion, justice and truth are, means that I can never again think of being Catholic in the terms in which I thought I understood it before taking a closer look.

I had begun the search with a degree of irritation about the handling of what I believed to be central issues in Catholicism, divorce, abortion and contraception. Now, I know these issues are important but could never again define being Christian, or Catholic, in terms of them. I grew up in a church and in a time where being Catholic was more likely to be defined negatively, and by reference to a narrow set of rules. We were against things, divorce, contraception, and abortion, and many other things. It has been personally liberating to discover what Catholicism is *for*.

And so theology, study and reflection on the Jesus of the Gospel accounts, went for me from being an interesting academic exercise to something that led me to live and work out of changed values. Far from leading to an acceptance of the *status quo* it gave new impetus to the very questions I had begun with all those years ago. What are we humans doing here? Where is meaning in our lives? On the one hand there is love. For example the love for particular other persons, or for humanity in general, gives meaning to our life, and is essentially connected to the love of God in all of creation, as Karl Rahner points out.[4] And alongside this there is the radical injustice in so many of our ways of organising ourselves and our world. The often unconscious bias which blinds me to my part in the suffering of others, shocked me and continues to shock me. The difference in regard for men and women, why there are rich and poor, loving others or acting destructively towards them, acceptance or rejection of aspects of self, all take new meaning in the light of the God question, and more specifically in the light of the person of Jesus Christ and the church which struggles, very often unsuccessfully, to be worthy of his name.

THE CHURCH NOW

The flaws in the church are painfully evident at the present time. At the level of institution the structures have been shown recently to be shockingly inadequate in the light of the needs of the people who are the church. The scandal that is clerical sexual abuse of children, and the even greater scandal of the way in which it has been handled by the church leadership, in many parts of the world, our own being a prime example, indicates that some of our church systems are out of control in the light of the needs of people today. All the big issues are connected in this one appalling episode in the current history of the church. Issues of justice and injustice, of power and control, of a clericalism run riot, issues of exploitation of fellow human beings, of an arrogance that, even if it is partly based on ignorance, is unacceptable and inexcusable, issues of human sexuality in all of its manifestations, converge in the emerging picture of the church in Ireland and in the world today. Add to this the issue of the morality of the exclusion of women from leadership and decision making roles, and its effects, issues of finance, and of an increasingly centralised and autocratic governing body, and you would wonder how any reasonable person of our time could want to belong to such a church. But the other side of the picture that is emerging gives the lie to such a judgement.

New ways of being in the church are evident in abundance. The relatively recent involvement of the laity in many aspects of the life of the church is showing the way forward. The rapidly decreasing numbers of ordained ministers and professed religious is making way for the possibility of men and women to work alongside them in countless new ways. This is what the teaching of Vatican Council II intended, and requires by the understanding of the implications of baptism of all the faithful.[5] Accelerated shortage of ordained and professed personnel seems to work better as an instigator of change than decades of tinkering at the edges of the structures with the new teaching. The traditional works of organising parishes, education, care of the sick, school and hospital and prison chaplaincy, care for people on the margins of societies, goes on, but with much teamwork between laity, religious and priests. This is not without its significant problems for relationships and structures. Agreement about ways of proceeding can be difficult to achieve. Lay men and women can be reluctant as well as over-keen to take on new responsibilities. Clergy can be over-keen as well as reluctant to let go of some responsibilities. New small groups and communities of lay people are being formed and provide a way of life and support for committed people that was not to be found in the older model of church. We are in a kind of twilight-zone, somewhere between the end of much of what has been and the beginnings of what will be. It may be true that many have left the church, but at the same time there is a great upsurge of interest in theology and spirituality. Men and women of all ages are taking courses in theology with the consequent broadening of perspectives.

Painstakingly, and for a considerable time now, the women and men who are feminist theologians have shown us how patriarchy and hierarchy have developed in the history of the church, neither of which is essential to its reason for being. Of course we need organisation, and leaders, and guardians of the tradition, but not solely drawn from such an exclusive and ex- cluding group. They have shown us how theology, studied and written by men only, at best has not been able to image God or tell the Christian story in a way that reflects adequately the hu- man searching for, and finding of, traces of God. And they have shown us how, at worst, some of the understandings handed down have contributed directly or indirectly to the exclusion of women from so much, and even to their oppression in many dif- ferent ways. They have uncovered missing voices and images and brought forward new ones, many of whom are still waiting to be recognised and fully included in the group of people of God who are the Catholic Church.

But women are not the only oppressed and excluded peo- ple. The liberation theologians have been teaching us for some time now that the emphasis on individual salvation and on per- sonal sin has not been adequate as an expression of the Chris- tian position in relation to our hope for humanity. We are individuals, but we belong also to various groups. Sin can be social too, when a group's systems and structures work for the benefit of the few at the cost of the wellbeing of the many. For a considerable time now, the liberation theologians have been pointing out the incompatibility between a professed Christian- ity and a knowing participation in systems and structures that keep down and undermine the full humanity of our fellow hu- man beings. There is a credibility problem with a professed Christianity and a deliberate ignoring of the plight of those on the edges of every society and country. Doing nothing, in the light of the need to change what works against the development of people and peoples, is not compatible with attempting to live in the spirit of Jesus that belonging in the church implies. But change happens slowly, it is a matter of taking small steps, do- ing what is possible, and, in a spirit of solidarity, accepting that we are in this together for the long haul.

The taking of small steps and solidarity for the long haul are needed within the church too. Here too are significant blocks to the work of the spirit of Jesus who came so that we might have life to the full. There are many justice issues to be addressed within the church. Who should have "life to the full"? Did he mean all, or just some? Did he mean children and women as well as men? Did he mean the poor as well as the materially rich? Did he mean the oppressed as well as the powerful? Who should be the leaders, the preachers and teachers? Who should be the guardians of orthodoxy, the authors of morality, the deciders of what way to proceed? Much theology has come from the top down. First principles, about God, or Jesus, or the church have directed theological reflection and so told us not just why we are here, and what we are for, but also what we should do. Today, not just the situation of the materially poor, but that of those on the edge for reasons of race, gender or sexual orientation, or those in prison or exiled, challenge many of the presumptions of traditional theology and demand that they be re-examined in the light of new information. And so it should be. We are not static beings, our ongoing learning and developing understanding of what it is to be human have everything to do with our understanding of God and how we might live the best lives we can in the light of that understanding. For this we need to hear many previously excluded groups, and to listen to and respect their sense of what is holy, their desires in respect of God.

THE CHURCH TO COME

Where are we headed? How will the church be in Ireland in the future?

Karl Rahner in *The Shape of the Church to Come* (1967) spoke of "a listening church", "a church of the grassroots", "a de-clericalised church". There are intimations already of the accuracy of his prediction. With more lay men and women taking up roles in different aspects of the life of the church, the face of the church is changing rapidly. Men and women, lay, religious and clergy together, are increasingly involved in the organising and running of the church. This is the priesthood of all the faithful being actualised. The issue of ministerial priesthood and compulsory celibacy is being addressed by the reality of the emerging situation of severely diminished numbers. It

is my belief that making celibacy a condition of priesthood devalues both celibacy and marriage. Yet an ordained priesthood
is of the essence of the group. Whether these should be men or
women, married or single, heterosexual or homosexual, celi-
bate or not, are important, but I think secondary issues. Does
this mean a married clergy and an end to celibacy? It seems
inevitable that some priests in the future will marry, and that
some married people will be ordained. Freely chosen celibacy,
celibacy as the sign of the truth of particular people, and their
way of being in relation to God, is of an order that most of us
cannot readily understand. Yet if we, who have chosen other
ways, listen closely to our own experience of love and intimacy
and sexual relationship we may hear what it is that celibacy is
saying. To be drawn to the One is not to reject the others, nor to
sacrifice close relationship with others. To be drawn to another
is not to reject the One, nor to sacrifice close relationship with
the One. Perhaps, at its most obvious, vowed celibacy means
being so engaged by the mystery of God that it is fundamentally all embracing of the person in their most radical self. It
needs no other explanation. Questions of availability for mission, or talk of heroic sacrifice, diminish its truth as far as I can
understand it. In this sense it is not a constraint, but rather a
freedom to be who you are in relation to God. Maybe in this
way we can understand talk of celibacy as a gift, in the same
way that others experience their marriage relationship, or other
committed relationship, as gift in its own right, and not for some
other purpose. Celibacy in this understanding would be the
starting point, the basis of a person's choice of way in the
church, and not the other way around with celibacy as an added
extra, whether understood positively or negatively. As such we
might all hope to understand better and so to value and support
people in the life they lead.

I would see this support, in the church of the future, extend-
ing to other groups. Current church discipline that excludes so
many, for example the divorced and remarried, from full participation in the Eucharist, is possibly a greater source of scandal than that which might result if they were invited to
participate fully. The Eucharist has a long and complicated history, both in terms of the reality and the understanding of that

reality. Various ongoing controversies, about who should be included, or not, and why, are indicative of that. But at base I believe it is simple, uncomplicated. Its meaning is a direct giving of self — a sharing of self for all — so that sins may be forgiven. But forgiven by whom? By the giver firstly, but maybe also by those who share in it. Can we share in it and not forgive? By sharing in it are we not forgiven? The Eucharist, the bread of life, is basic, the staple, for this life to be lived by all in the spirit of Christ. So it is reminder-sign, and spiritual reality. The spiritual presence of Christ, we believe is in the bread, but also in all who share in it, the group gathered in his name. Increasingly the exclusion of particular groups from sharing fully seems not to fit with this understanding. The language of welcome and inclusion is often talked, but too often it is accompanied by behaviour patterns ensuring that the experience is the opposite. I hope and believe that, in the church of the future, the understanding of Eucharist, rather than laws about marriage or annulment, or membership of another denomination or faith group, will mean that at the eucharistic celebration the words of Jesus, "Take this all of you and eat it", will mean exactly that, and all present will know themselves included.

Another aspect of the church of the future must be more inter-faith learning at grassroots level, and more exchange of understandings of the different ways to God. The "listening church" that Karl Rahner spoke of will be enriched by hearing from people of the many different faith communities now represented in Ireland. One of the many benefits of the opening out of Ireland to newcomers from diverse cultures is the possibility of coming to know and respect other faiths in a new way. It is good that we have had religious education programmes that include study of other religions but interpersonal encounters and shared programmes on different understandings of the meaning of life must be of greater benefit to everyone.

The church is the People of God. It is not static but a dynamic entity. Believing in the presence of God and the spirit of Christ in the church, we need not be afraid of the changes that are already here, nor of the unknown future which is coming to meet us. It is exciting and a privilege to take part in the history as it unfolds, to be a link in the long line of Catholics attempting to be faithful to their truth. I end by coming almost full circle and recording gratitude to the many inspiring and inspired teachers of philosophy and theology from whom it has been my privilege to learn. In their persons and manner of sharing their faith and learning they have provided authentic links with a tradition and pointers to a future that is open and welcoming to the radical changes that will be at the basis of the next phase of our journey.

Notes

[1] Two works in particular were foundational. *Insight. A Study of Human Understanding.* New York, Philosophical Library, 1957, and *Method in Theology*, London, Darton, Longman & Todd, 1972.

[2] See, for example, Alister McGrath, *Christian Theology* (Oxford: Blackwell, 1994), pp. 105–7.

[3] Juan Luis Segundo, *The Liberation of Theology* (Dublin: Gill and Macmillan, 1997), pp. 27–34.

[4] Karl Rahner, "Marriage as a Sacrament", *Theological Investigations,* (New York: Herder and Herder, 1973), X, pp. 199–221.

[5] John Paul II, *Christifideles Laici* (London: CTS, 1988), n. 14.

Chapter 8

LANDSCAPE AND INSCAPE: A LABYRINTHINE LOOK AT LANDSCAPE, MYTH AND MEANING

Ellen O'Malley-Dunlop

INTRODUCTION: ROOTS IN IRISH MYTH

Tomás Ó Cathasaigh, writing about mythology for the *Crane Bag* in 1978, wrote:

> . . . it is not primarily as a quarry for modern creative writers that Irish mythology lays claim upon our attention, but rather as a rich and complex body of material which is there and which calls for elucidation and interpretation. It is in that mythology that we can discover the native ideology of Ireland, for although the early Irish material includes a valuable Wisdom Literature the abstract formulation of philosophical and theological theories was not the Irish way. It was in their myths that they explored the nature of men and the gods and a central task of criticism must be to uncover and re-state in abstract terms the configuration of the ideological patterns which underlie the myths.[1]

What Ó Cathasaigh is clearly encouraging us to do is to discover, explore, uncover and to use as our material, the rich and unique body of lore and legend that is Irish mythology. Our task is surely more than the thorough textual criticism of the scholar. It is the task of rediscovering and re-experiencing our unique "Irish way" of making sense of the world.

This is a story of a labyrinthine journey looking at myth, meaning and landscape. As in any journey we pick up other stories and experiences on the way. We realise, as reader or participant or listener, that in our journey towards meaning, towards a meaningful life, we have potentially an ongoing dance between our inscape and our landscape. In Ireland, as we struggle with our faith and our philosophy, we have a great abundance by way of myth and legend and a great richness by way of landscape to help us in our quest.

As long ago as 1725, Giambattista Vico claimed that "the first science to be learned should be mythology or the interpretation of fables". It was with this in mind that I enrolled as a postgraduate student in the Irish Folklore Department of University College Dublin and there I found a feast of material. As well as the manuscripts that are thankfully available in the many libraries both at home and abroad, one need only look at our filmmakers, read our poets and novelists, philosophers, theologians to know that our myths are the underlying source that keep bubbling through to the surface demanding expression. Even before I encountered the Folklore Department with its wonderful Manuscript and Schools' collections, I encountered the characters and/or archetypes from our rich mythological tradition in my work as a psychotherapist and group analyst. The lived tradition and imaginative weavings of our myths and legends are impressing themselves upon individuals and groups of individuals who have the desire and the curiosity to cross the threshold into the imagination and the world of dreams, to examine and explore their interpretations and their meaning. Our myths and legends are very much alive in the Irish psyche.

The experience of working with this material, the inscape of the psyche, has been an exciting odyssey and continually opens up into vistas that can be unwittingly familiar and sometimes terrifyingly challenging but always rewarding and, without doubt, food for the soul. Having encountered the characters from our myths in the dreams of individuals and having worked with them in the way Ó Cathasaigh suggested, for example uncovering the underlying meanings, has led me into other areas and other questions. If these mythological characters have meaning in the individual context, what meaning might the myths themselves have for society today? This essay is also about one way that a group of fellow travellers sought to "uncover" and "restate" their ideological patterns for lives lived in today's world. This exploration of the Irish myths began ten years ago and continues in the form of the Bard Summer School, which will be described later on. First let us take a look at the connections between the dream and the myth. To do this we will take a look at the great work that was initiated by Freud and developed further by Jung.

FREUD AND JUNG

In the late 1800s Freud wrote his groundbreaking work *The Interpretation of Dreams*. It was Carl Jung who then extended our understanding of the dream to include "collective unconscious" material that he termed "archetypal themes". Jung organised his ideas about dreams into a general theory but did not write an equivalent to Freud's *Interpretation of Dreams*. What he did do, in the 18 volumes of his *Collected Works*, was to weave his work and ideas about dreams throughout his whole life's work which reflects the huge acknowledgement of the importance of dreams and their interpretation. He never considered his formulations final so he never felt compelled to organise his body of concepts. Nevertheless, the sum total of his work on dreams comprises a highly developed and clinically well-tested theory.

Freud and Jung disagreed over the question of manifest and latent dream content. Jung did not regard the dream as a potentially deceptive message requiring careful decoding. He wrote:

> I take the dream for what it is. The dream is such a difficult and complicated thing that I do not dare to make any assumptions about its possible cunning or its tendency to deceive. The dream is a natural occurrence, and there is no earthly reason why we should assume it is a crafty device to lead us astray.[2]

Jung, in the early 1900s, said:

> To reflect on myths is to reflect on oneself. I had to know what unconscious or preconscious myth was forming me, from what rhizome I sprang.

Daryl Sharp, in her book *Jungian Psychology Unplugged* in the 1990s, reiterates this same sentiment:

> Knowledge of oneself is a result of looking in two directions at once. In order to know ourselves we need both relationships with other people and the mirror of the unconscious. Dreams provide that mirror.

In looking at what myths and dreams have in common we can add that myths provide the mirror to our collective unconscious. We can look at myths and dreams as tales from and about psychological life, the subjective not objective life.

> For it is in the dream that the dreamer himself performs as one image among others and where it can legitimately be shown that the dreamer is in the image rather than the image in the dreamer.[3]

And indeed the individual is in the myth rather than just the myth in the individual.

Jung and Freud worked primarily with Greek myths in their work. Irish myths are very different. Because the Irish myths remained in the oral tradition until they were written down by the Christian monks and their successors (almost a thousand years later than in Greece) they are very different in quality from the Greek myths. They are less linear, less ordered and more richly imaginative. In this sense they are very much like dreams. Jung held that the dream is both an individual and a collective phenomenon, that is, it can be derived from our personal unconscious life (which in turn results from our personal history) or it can be formed from our history as a species, the collective history of the race, and in these situations we have what are termed "archetypal dreams".[4]

Archetypes refer to patterns of instinctual knowing with which we are born; they are not something we acquire. These patterns of knowing are like the instinctual migratory patterns in birds. They are derived from the repeated, universal experiences that human beings have faced such as birth, death, separation, rivalry, relationships, youth, old age, etc. They form the bedrock of the individual psyche and clearly provide the link between myths and dreams. This is put very well by E.R. Dodds when he states that myths are the "dream-thinking of the people, as the dream is the myth of the individual". Peter O'Connor, in his book *Beyond the Mist*, writes:

> Myths therefore are the social equivalent of archetypal dreams and invariably attend to the universal themes that confront human beings. Mythology as James Hillman asserts, is the "psychology of antiquity and psychology and mythology of modernity".

So it is with this backdrop of information and wonderings that we set off on the odyssey of finding out if these links with the dream and the myth have any validity. To give form to this my husband and I have developed a one-week experience to explore the contemporary relevance of myth and legend to make sense of our modern world. The week's exploration includes the group's experience as well as the individual's experience, and this inclusion gives an extra context for exploring the cultural and social levels of understanding and meaning of the myths.

THE BARD

Myths once occupied a central role in societies and were a way people made sense of their world. When scientists and historians pointed out that these myths were not true, people often felt cheated, so much so that the word myth has come to mean nonsense, or that which is not true. The Bard Summer School was set up ten years ago with the explicit aim to explore Irish myths and to ask not whether "is it true?" but "is it useful?" To do so we look on myth as a language, as a tool, to help make sense of the complexities, changes and challenges of the modern world. In this interpretation, myth can be seen as a process, as a description of a journey. Myth reflects back the world; it occasionally points, but it does not conclude. It is the individual's and the group's task to draw their own conclusions.

Each year participants have come from Ireland and from different countries all over the world to the Bard Summer School. The week's experience has taken us to places in ourselves that we never knew existed and expanded us in ways we never thought possible. To symbolise what we were attempting to do during the week a local sculptor, Wayne Harlow, created a sculpture for us out of 10,000-year-old bog oak. The end result is pleasing to the eye, contemporary and provocative. We call the creation The Bard, the bard of old being the story-teller, the bearer of tradition. The purpose of the week is to examine and to explore the territory of our collective unconscious through its expression in Irish myths in particular. We were also curious to observe and recognise the layers of meaning that can be accessed for us as individuals and for us in our wider contexts in our contemporary worlds. So like our sculptor who worked with the ancient bog oak and created our Bard sculpture, which is both ancient and contemporary, we work with the old material of the myths and see what emerges for us for today's world.

During a Bard week we focus on an Irish myth and a related theme. In the past few years we have looked at *The Pursuit of Diarmuid and Grainne* with the theme of love and betrayal. That year (1998), the analyses and retellings were full of death imagery as if we were about to experience death, which of course we were in that the death of the century was imminent. The experience of the explored theme manifesting itself at a societal level either simultaneously or soon afterwards is a pattern that we have observed over the course of many of the Summer schools.

At another workshop we explored *Midir and Etain* with the theme of transitions and transformation. It was quite striking how in that year one of the underlying themes of incest was side-stepped and avoided though very much present in the myth. Very shortly afterwards the whole institutional abuse scandals began to emerge.

We have explored *The Táin* with its theme of wasteland and abundance and pondered on the Curse of Macha, the curse that in times of crises means that all the men of Ulster suffer a sleeping sickness and are immobilised. Cu Chulainn was the only one left to defend Ulster because he was just seventeen and still a boy, so not affected by the curse. We discovered that Cu Chulainn was used as a symbol for both sides of the conflict in Northern Ireland. During that week other sides of Cu Chulainn began to emerge as well as the "Terminator"[5] side that is so often the only association with this great hero. For example, time and thought was given to the manner in which he was conceived and what that might mean. He is at once the son of a god, Lugh, and of a human father, Sualdaim Mac Roich. During his life he didn't have contact with either father. What affect did this have on him? He was separated from his mother, Dechtine, when as a young boy he went to Tara and was then sent to Scotland to learn the art of warfare from the famous warrior queen Scathach. His relationship with Ferdia and the pain of having to fight to the death one he loved were also considered. The possible homosexual undercurrents were explored. Links were made to current social trends of one-parent families and what this might mean in the longer term for society as a whole and society's attitude to homosexuality.

To work this way with myth requires participants to be open to myth as allegory. The allegorical approach was of course widespread in the medieval and renaissance periods. Both religious and pagan stories were widely accepted as allegories of the inner life, as well as of the cultural and social life. Once this hurdle has been overcome it is the participant's and group's task to create meaning. As we have seen, they found the myth a powerful way to explore a variety of social, cultural and indeed personal issues. Once the group or individual is open to the allegorical approach there is every likelihood that the outer world, the landscape, can also be viewed allegorically. In a sense, everything speaks.

THE ISLAND

As part of the odyssey we chose Clare Island in Clew Bay, County Mayo to be the venue for our Summer School. Why Clare Island? Clare Island was the ancestral home of the illustrious 16th. century ancestor of the O'Malleys, Grace O'Malley, the Pirate Queen. She was a remarkable woman, not only for her own time but for any time. It is reputed that she is buried on the island and that her remains are interred in the 11th century ruined Cistercian Abbey. Like many of our historical characters, Grace O'Malley, through the stories passed on mainly via the oral tradition (her life and times were not recorded in the

Annals of the Four Masters but this was redressed by Anne Chambers),[6] has taken on a mythological form and there are those who believe she was a mythical and not a historical person. We chose Clare Island for lots of reasons, among them its physical beauty, its remoteness, its antiquity, its tranquility to name but a few of its many qualities. We also chose to go to an island so that we could experience the actual physical leaving behind of our ordinary every day life on the mainland to enter more fully into engaging with the otherworld, the inner worlds, both the personal and the collective.

We were not alone in acknowledging the rich sources of tradition and enquiry that are part of an exploration of island life. Robert Lloyd Praeger, the renowned naturalist, conducted a survey of all forms of life on Clare Island from plant to human life in the early nineteenth century. The Royal Irish Academy repeated this survey in the 1990s, which was instigated by the good works of the Centre for Island Studies founded by Ciara Cullen and Peter Gill. These surveys of Clare Island can be viewed as a microcosm of life on the mainland. They are unique in that the studies looked at almost every angle of life on the island. The later survey is in the process of being published but Praeger's survey, called "A Biological Survey of Clare Island County Mayo Ireland and of the Adjoining District", was published between 1911 and 1915 in the *Proceedings of the Royal Irish Academy* and comprised an impressive 67 reports.[7] Praeger found Clare Island an irresistible object of study, an opportunity to observe his subject, as the scientist sees his subject, under the microscope.

The Congested Districts Board bought the island from the last landlord in 1895. The Board first experimented with striping (re-apportioning the island from the rundale system of farming into new farms separated by walls and fencing) the land on Clare Island before it was implemented on the mainland and the islanders became landowners buying the newly striped and fenced holdings from the Board.

Clare Island is one of the largest islands in Clew Bay, which boasts 365 islands, "an island for each day of the year" according to the locals. When driving into Westport town en route to Clare Island, the sight of the Holy Mountain Croagh Patrick, which presents itself (when the weather is clear, or as a woman once told me, when the mountain wants to be seen) on the left of the horizon, and Clare Island sphinx-like and jutting up from the sea, on the right of the horizon, is transporting. The view of these two ancient symbols never fails to touch the soul; Croagh Patrick with its worn paths from thousands of years of pilgrims climbing its summit to repent and seek forgiveness, to celebrate and give thanks. Its mood ranging from mystical to menacing and all the tones in between, and Clare Island magical, timeless and with its own pervasive sense of permanence.

CROAGH PATRICK

Long before the Christians adopted the tradition from the pagan god Crom, Croagh Patrick was a very important site to the ancients of Ireland. In an 11th century text,[8] Crom is called Crom Cruach and is described as an idol of the pagan Irish. He is also associated with Patrick in an earlier 9th century biography of Patrick as Cenn Cruaich. Legend tells how St. Patrick demolished the statue of Cenn Cruaich in Magh Sleacht (the plain of Tullyhaw, County Cavan) and it sunk into the ground. Here Cenn Cruach is seen as the anti-Christ. The name Cenn Cruaich, or Crom Dubh as it became later, has been taken to mean "black stoop" and "dark croucher", an image of the devil. In later medieval legends Crom Dubh is portrayed as a great sinner who after his death was saved by Patrick from being carried away by demons. According to the legend, Patrick saved him because each year Crom had given a bullock to the poor to help them through difficult times, and so Patrick was rewarding his good deeds. In another legend, Crom gives a cauldron as a gift of thanks to Patrick and the saint shows that his thanks, written on a piece of paper, outweighs Crom's gift on a scales. Crom is so over awed by this demonstration that he is converted to Christianity before his death.

More ancient imagery presents the encounter between Patrick and Crom Dubh at the festival of Lughnasa. This festival, which celebrated the ripening of the corn and the weaning of calves and lambs, was celebrated on the Sunday nearest the 1st of August[9] which was known in most of county Mayo as "Crom

Dubh's Sunday". Since Lughnasa is a harvest festival dedicated
to the Celtic God Lugh (possessor of all the arts) it could be
concluded that the mythical encounter of Patrick and Crom
Dubh represented an earlier encounter between Balor of the
Evil Eye and Lugh[10] (the bright one) during the great primordial battle in Irish mythology, the Battle of Moytura, representing the battle between good and evil.[11]

THE END OF A TRADITION

More recently, Clare Island has experienced the end of an era
pertaining to the spiritual life of its inhabitants, namely that the
last remaining priest living on the island was moved and has
not and will not be replaced. Nowadays a priest comes once a
week, weather permitting, to say Mass and administer the Sac-
raments, while on other occasions the islanders themselves
conduct the rituals. Could this be a template for the future of
religious ritual and spiritual welfare on the mainland of Ireland?

Already this journey across Ireland en route to Clare Island
is bringing us into another world. The otherworld as our ancestors called it, was always close at hand with only a veil separat-
ing the two worlds. As we draw nearer to Clare Island this veil
begins to drop slowly but surely, encouraged by the landscape
and the stories. Clare Island is a place at the edge, a liminal
place, at the boundaries of the known world, indeed as my-
thologists tell us, a place of transformation and change. This
moving to the edge is a recurring theme in European mythology. The Greek heroes Jason, Perseus, and Theseus all travelled to the edge. In ancient times Perseus travelled to the
westernmost extremity of the earth. We are told, "he found
monsters with locks of serpents whom none could look upon
without perishing". As we are on the periphery of Ireland and
of Europe, we find ourselves in the place where the Celtic and
the Christian traditions meet. We immediately encounter this
meeting ground with the wonderful sight of Croagh Patrick's
powerful presence. The landscape sometimes forces itself upon
us, gently presents itself or doesn't show itself at all. However,
no matter how we experience it, gently or startlingly, it is for-

ever there. This sense of permanence has an encouraging and comforting feel.

What else do we know about liminal space? It is a space where anything is possible. As Colin Smythe[12] tells us, Pagan hero or Christian saint set off in a small boat, guided solely by the wind or the waves. They went in search of the Land of Delight, Mag Mell, Tir na nOg, or as in later Christian versions, a paradise promised by Christ. The inspiration for these voyages is to be found in a body of literature called "immrama", which tells about visits to otherworldly islands. Here we are no longer confronted with an ordinary dimension of existence but rather with the unfamiliar shapes and figures of a mythological order. In Celtic myth there are no sharp boundaries between the two worlds, between what is and what can be, between perception and imagination. Death is an attribute of life and life of death. Clare Island awaits!

To get to Clare Island one has to go to Roonagh pier about six miles from Louisburgh and take a boat to cross the often-treacherous five-mile sea journey to the island. On calm beautiful days with the dolphins accompanying the boat and performing for the traveller, it can be difficult to imagine the rough sea days. Whatever the weather, on reaching the island one is immediately struck by the calm of the place and the comforting presence of Knockmore, the 1600-foot mountain to the North West which has featured in many of the paintings of Tony O'Malley.

During World War II Clare Island had its own unique experiences of the awful consequences of war. There were many bodies washed ashore, victims of sea warfare. These bodies were identified and sent back to their families to be buried. One man, a young soldier whose name was Private Tweed, had no family to claim him and it was decided that he should be buried on the island. The priest at the time refused to bury him inside the consecrated graveyard ground because he was not a Catholic. Instead, he was buried outside the walls much to the annoyance of many islanders who refused to go to Mass for the duration of that priest's time on the island. In 2000 the last priest on the island, Fr Ned, with the help of an island man Myles Ruddy, quietly took down stone by stone the old wall of the graveyard and extended the walls to include Private Tweed's grave. The islanders erected a tombstone to commemorate him.

This priest was a man who seemed to have touched everyone on the island from the very old to the very young, from the very religious to the very sceptical. My first experience of his homilies, which he delivered not from the altar but from the body of the church, was an evening when I slipped unnoticed, or so I thought, into the first vacant seat, as I was late. I was taken aback by the quiet "you're welcome" from the man who then continued with his homily. The attention this man commanded in that small church tenderly decorated and candle-lit by the islanders was remarkable. His passion seemed gentle and fierce at the same time. He told stories to illustrate his points and you knew he was always well-prepared. That night, to demonstrate a point from the gospel reading about the dangers of holding on to possessions, he, holding firmly on to one of the seats in the church said, "as long as I hold onto this seat I am as much a prisoner of this seat as it is of me". I never missed a homily after that and I was never disappointed. I watched in amazement at the ways this man prepared the people to administer to themselves and to each other when he was gone. He instilled in everyone a sense of the importance of ritual during the short two years he spent on the island. He acted as a bridge between the ancient and the Christian worlds that are so evident on the island, by reconnecting and resurrecting the old rituals and the pilgrimages to the holy island of Caher, among many other events and commemorations.

> One thing Ireland does not possess is wilderness. No area has remained untouched, no field unmarked, no landscape untransformed by human hand. The haunting beauty of the desolate western landscape has been intensively influenced by successive generations. Nowhere is this more applicable than on Clare Island. What one initially perceives to be a wilderness is instead a palimpsest of 5,000 to 7,000 years of human habitation.[13]

What better place to go to explore some of the internal topography (the inscape) of the Irish psyche and put under the microscope a chosen myth. Where better in the haunting outer landscape of the island to explore the desolate wilderness and landscape (inscape) of the human spirit.

THE BARD WEEK

In conversation with Richard Kearney, Paul Ricoeur said:

> Modern man can neither get rid of myth nor take it at its face value. Myth will always be with us, but we must always approach it critically.[14]

This is what we attempt to do for the week: approach the myth critically from a variety of perspectives — from the literary perspective, the psychological, the historical, the philosophical, the storyteller and the poetic. We invite scholars to give presentations and we have workshops where we explore the myth in greater depth and detail. We use a variety of approaches. From the psychological perspective we look at the myth as if it were a dream and associate and elucidate and develop the themes.

The myth can be likened to an island, in that it is a story told within a boundary with a beginning, a middle and an end. It can be viewed as holding all of life in the contained space of the story itself, albeit at the symbolic level. Clare Island has lent itself so generously and favourably to studies and surveys over the last few centuries, being a place where man has lived and loved for over 5,000 years. The land and its people welcome us each year and support and contribute to our explorations. Now we will look at one example from our enquiries and draw some conclusions from the experiences of working with, retelling and analysing one of the Irish myths.

To get a flavour of what happens we will take one story, *The Fate of the Children of Lir*, and follow its progress throughout the week. The week begins with everyone crossing to the island on the ferry. As the ferry is a people ferry and not a car ferry one has to leave one's car on the mainland and bring just the essentials for the week. Sometimes this can have an unsettling effect for some of the participants. It can be experienced as a letting go of the familiar and a moving into uncertainty. This can often move the individual into a place where they can ask some of the bigger questions like where do we come from? Where are we going? What's it all about? I am reminded of the Seamus Heaney poem[15] as the participants set out there is

> A farewell to surefootedness, a pitch
> Beyond our usual hold upon ourselves.

And the promise of:

> And what went on kept going, from grip to give,
> The narrow milky way in the black ice,
>
> The race-up, the free passage and return —
> It followed on itself like a ring of light
> We knew we'd come through and kept sailing towards.

Our week began with a general welcoming ceremony so that the group and the islanders might meet one another over a glass of wine. School proper began the next morning with the explorations of the myth. (The group always works in the round unless they are working in breakout sessions. The circle works as a container and the space in the centre becomes a safe place in the week for the group and the individuals to explore freely with each other.) Each participant had a copy of the story/myth from Marie Heaney's *Over Nine Waves*. There were other versions of the myth and for *The Fate of the Children of Lir* we used the fifteenth-century literary text *Oidhe Chloinne Lir Siosana*.[16]

After introductions each participant listed three to five stories/myths that had been significant in their life and shaped what was important and meaningful to them individually. This was followed by a story-telling session and the group listened to a member of the team tell the story based on the old text. Some of the details they heard for the first time as the Marie Heaney retelling does not have all the motifs that are in the original text.

The following is a synopsis of the *Fate of the Children of Lir*: The story tells of how the Tuatha De Danann chose Badhbh Dearg as their king. Lir of Sodh Fionnachaidh was angered because he had hoped to be the one to be king. To placate him Bodhbh offered him one of his foster-daughters in marriage as his first wife had died. His new wife Aobh bore him two sets of twins. The first set was a girl named Fionnghula and a boy named Aodh. The second set was two boys, Conn and Fiachra. Aobh died on the birth of the second set of twins and Lir was once again without a wife. Lir was distraught but Bodhbh offered him Aoife, his second foster-daughter, as his wife and Lir was happy to accept her. Everyone loved the children and so did Aoife in the beginning but she grew very jealous of Lir's affection for his children and she planned to get rid of them.

When it came to killing them Aoife could not bring herself to do the bad deed. Instead she struck them with a magic wand and turned them into swans. She cursed them to spend 300 years on Loch Daibhreach (Lake Derrabarragh in County Westmeath), 300 years on Sruth na Maoile (the Sea of Moyle between Ireland and Scotland) and 300 years off Iorras Domhnann (Erris, County Mayo). When Bodhbh discovered what had been done he changed Aoife into a demon, in which form she wandered the air forever. After their long imprisonment the swans flew to Inis Gluaire (an island in the bay of Erris) when they found their father's Sidh (home) empty and abandoned. On Inis Gluaire they met the Christian missionary St. Mochaomhog who treated them with great kindness. Not long afterwards the king of Connacht Lairgnean married the daughter of the king of Munster and her name was Deoch. She had heard of the swans and she requested them as her wedding present. Lairgnean tried to take them from Mochaomhog but their period of enchantment had come to an end and they turned into three withered old men and an old woman. The saint baptised them and they were buried as requested by Fionnghuala.

The group then had the opportunity of discussing the telling and describing their emotional reactions to it. One of the stronger responses was the expression of anger relating to the inclusion at the end of the story of the monk Mochaomhog who baptised the children so that they could go to Heaven when they died. The group felt that it was incongruous with what had gone before in the story and felt it was an example of the Church's interference. They felt it had been tacked on to the story and was possibly done by the Cleric Scribe and this was expanded upon with associations from contemporary society.

Michael Gibbons, the archaeologist, then brought the group on a metaphorical journey into the landscape of Clare Island from cairn to court tomb to *fulachta fiadh*[17] and on to Inis Gloire where the Children of Lir spent their last days.

In the afternoon the group explored the characters of the story in more detail. They read prepared profiles and received visual images that captured the values and personalities of the characters. The Children of Lir covered a 900-year span and in this time there were great changes in world view. Based on this knowledge the next exercise invited the individuals in groups of four to take a look at Ireland and the world from the perspective of key events in history and culture that has shaped their lives and meaning. The day ended with a group session where individuals expressed some of their delight with the material and also some of their concerns. One of the Irish participants found it difficult to accept that people from other cultures would be capable of working with an Irish myth. There were representatives from France, England, Japan, Barbados, America and Ireland at this year's school. The participants went on an island tour and met later for dinner and an informal singsong.

Day 2 began with a look at how story-telling works with an input from one of the team members on how stories create meaning through difference. There are two types — essential opposition (agon) and the emotional ups and downs (reversals). It is interesting to observe how when one enters into the world of a story one starts to live the tugs and pulls and polarities of the emerging theme. These were then mapped by the group working in pairs and using *The Children of Lir* story as the template. John Moriarty, writer and philosopher, spoke on the theme of exile and return and took the group through the story as well as connecting *The Children of Lir* story to other migratory legends, i.e. *The Swan Children* and the *Seal Woman*. The group then went further into the story and prepared a session where the characters of the story talked to each other. At this stage everyone was fully engaged and there was a lot of energy in the group. After another session with John Moriarty the participants were treated to an evening of story-telling, music and dance from the islanders.

Day three brought the group into the story from the perspective of the characters, the insights from the character discussions of the previous day and connections they were making to contemporary issues, from the pagan/Christian, power/business and legal perspectives. Professor Daithí Ó hÓgáin from the Folklore Department of UCD developed the connections to the European migratory legends and brought us further into the literary text and illustrated how connections were made from the dialect in the text, its origins and its style. In the afternoon the group broke into subgroups and looked at the story from the perspective of frameworks of culture change, i.e. Renaissance, Reformation and Enlightenment. The group then began the process of preparing for the re-telling of the story. In the evening we celebrated with the islanders with a feast of poetry from West of Ireland poets Ned Crosby and Ger Reidy and our own poet Karina Tynan.

On day four we began with reflections on all the experiences to date. We did exercises where we looked at what we wanted to hold on to from our past, what we wanted to let go of and what new vision we aspired to, as individuals and for our society. In the afternoon there were three sub-groups and each group presented their own retelling of *The Children of Lir*.

There is not enough space here to detail everything that happened but I will endeavour to give a brief synopsis of each re-telling to give a flavour of the culmination of the week's work.

Group 1 chose to begin their retelling story on the Sea of Moyle where the children suffered tremendous agony and torture. Their presentation was in the form of a mini-drama with narrator, mime and chorus. They developed the story around the power that was invested in the "wand" of Aoife and Bodh and presented a drama where they enacted the children's anger with Aoife and then returned the symbol of power to the earth goddess where it was buried forever. Aoife was forgiven and transformed from the evil person to a kind warm woman. They delivered a chorus which went thus:

> Take this great power and energy
> which has destroyed us.
> Hold it, as we hand it over.
> Bury it deep within your earth,
> Transforming it and us.
> So that we may draw again from this power
> For love and life.

The second group used the dance format and involved the whole group in a circle dance with pipe and fiddle music. The theme of the dance was separation and return.

The third presentation used the drama format. There was a narrator who told the story with a different twist. They incorporated a new plot whereby the children escaped the evil plotting of Aoife and managed to build a whole new life for themselves. They had Aoife and Lir living on together and having other children. They then had the three boys tell their story and had a ritual where they released Fionnuala from the responsibility of looking after them.

On the last day each presentation was analysed by the group under the following headings:

- What was the essence of your group's retelling?

- What message/effect did you want to have?

- What was the central agon?

- How do you feel about the re-telling? What changes if any would you make?

CONCLUSION

We have taken a journey across Ireland to Clare Island where we had a whistle-stop tour of a week spent in another world, in the world of imagination and soul-making.

What I have described is the importance of developing a new context where the insights from Jungian psychology, philosophy, folklore and archeology and the insights from mythology are woven into a tapestry that serves as a template and a mirror for the questions and wonderings that have always brought us to the edge of our knowing and that serve us as important reminders as we encounter complex modern dilemmas that can stretch our incredulity as we live out lives.

James Hillman, when writing about dreams, says we must "befriend" our dreams and by this he means to participate in them, to understand, play with, live with, carry and become familiar with, as one would do with a friend. He says

> As I grow familiar with my dreams I grow familiar with my inner world. Who lives in me? What inscapes are mine? What is recurrent and therefore what keeps coming back to reside in me?[18]

I will not analyse the different retellings of the story because I believe that it is in the experience of the encounter with the myth that the magic of the unfolding happens. Each individual member has their own experience and their own unique understanding of the experience in the context of their lives in their own communities. There was no doubt at the end of this week on Clare Island that change had taken place and that each and everyone of the participants and course facilitators were touched by land, sea, sky and the otherworld.

I now invite you to reread the text with soft eyes and encounter your own curiosity and meet your own questions.

Notes

[1] Ó Cathasaigh, Tomás (1978), "Between God and Man: The Hero of Irish Tradition", in Hederman/Kearney (eds.) *The Crane Bag of Irish Studies Mythology*, Vol. 2, Nos. 1&2. Blackwater Press, p. 220.

[2] Jung, Carl (1981), *The Collected Works,* Vol. 2, London: Routledge & Kegan Paul, p. 4.

[3] Hillman, James (1985), *Archetypal Psychology,* Dallas: Spring Publications, p. 6.

[4] O'Connor, Peter (2000), *Beyond the Myst,* London: Orion, p. 5.

[5] Arnold Swarzenegger: *Terminator* films.

[6] Chambers, Anne (1998) *Granuaile: The Life and Times of Grace O'Malley,* Dublin: Wolfhound. First edition, 1979.

[7] Praeger, R.L. (1915) *Clare Island Survey,* General Summary, Section 68, Dublin: Royal Irish Academy, pp. 1-15.

[8] Ó hÓgáin, Daithí (1991), *Myth Legend and Romance*, New York: Prentice Hall, p. 128.

[9] Lunasa is the Irish for the month of August.

[10] According to Latin scholars who argue that Lugh is cognate with the Latin word *lux* meaning light.

[11] Ó hÓgáin, Daithí, *Myth Legend and Romance,* p. 373.

[12] Smythe, Colin (1973), *Voyages of Saint Brendan.*1973.

[13] Cullen, Ciara & Gill, Peter, *Clare Island Series Studying an Island* Series 5, p. 2.

[14] Kearney, Richard, interview with Paul Ricoeur (1978), "Myth as the Bearer of Possible Worlds", in Hederman/Kearney (eds.) *The Crane Bag of Irish Studies Mythology*, Vol. 2, Nos. 1 and 2. Blackwater Press, p. 260.

[15] Heaney, Seamus (1991), *Seeing Things* London: Faber & Faber, *xxviii*, p. 86.

[16] (Editions) O'Curry, Eugene (1927) *Atlantis,* 4, 113-57; Sean Ua Ceallaigh, pp. 42-64.

[17] Bronze Age cooking site.

[18] Hillman, James (1989), *A Blue Fire*, London: Routledge, p. 141.

Chapter 9

THAT ALL MAY BE ONE

Patrick Treacy

In the mythological story of the Garden of Eden, Adam and Eve
eat from the tree of knowledge. At that moment, they become
aware of the duality of life, of good and evil, birth and death,
love and fear. Having gained this knowledge, they experience
the "Fall" or the loss of innocence in that they now see themselves as separated from God, outside of the divine union which
they had enjoyed. They move into the field of time and space
where life is scattered and fragmented and where they struggle
with duality and a sense of separateness from God. All of their
central relationships become fragmented — their relationship
with God, with themselves, with each other and with nature. At
this point, the centre no longer holds.

Against this background of the Jewish faith, the death and
resurrection of Jesus Christ is the creation of a new union between God and man — the mending of the wound of Judaism.
His death, which was marked upon the Cross or meeting point,
can be seen as the moment when all things are drawn back together as one and the creation of a new centre which holds between God and man. Just as eating from the tree of knowledge
marks the beginning of disintegration, the raising of Jesus on
the cross marks the crux for the re-integration of all of life,
drawn magnetically to the love of God, revealed in this Easter
event.

The centrality of Jesus Christ is that His being, or more particularly, the love from His being, re-integrates or brings together that which has been disintegrated at the "Fall". He
gathers together all that has been scattered. His being "lifted
up" on the cross, which we remember at each Eucharist, draws
us like a magnetic force to the centre, where we become aware
of the full extent of the love which He reveals.

> And I, when I am lifted up from the earth, will draw all peo-
> ple to myself. (John 12:32.)

This theme of Jesus drawing all things together again, by at-
tracting them to himself, runs through St John's Gospel. It is a
restoration of unity and harmony, which fulfils a God-inspired
dream had by the Prophets. This dream was that the Messiah
would re-establish the order which there was between the different parts of creation at the beginning. Just as the bronze ser-
pent which Moses lifted up before the people healed them, so
too the lifting of the body and blood of Jesus Christ draws us to
His healing love.

> And as Moses lifted up the serpent in the wilderness, even
> so must the Son of Man be lifted up, that whosoever believ-
> eth in him should not perish, but have eternal life. For God
> so loved the world, that He gave His only begotten Son (John
> 3:14–16).

When the love of God, made visible in the cross, ceases to be
the centre of our lives, what binds us together loses its hold and
we disintegrate or fall apart. In this era, we have also eaten
from the tree of knowledge. We live in the information age, a
time of enormous technological advancement and innovation.
Yet, as with each stage of progression, there is also a new level
of complexity to the problems which this advancement entails.
The contemporary problem is the fragmentation or disintegration of central relationships that are essential for human happiness and spiritual growth.

Even fragmentation at the most superficial level gives rise to
profound problems. This is found in the breakdown of the relationship between each of us and the central institutions of society. Public cynicism with the social institutions of the legal

system, "the Church" and the political system is a daily theme in the discourse of Western society. The complaint made against all three institutions is essentially the same — a loss of belief in their integrity and a loss of trust in their concern for the common good and the public interest.

While this problem is of great magnitude, it belies a deeper fragmentation in our relationships. For beneath the loss of connection to our social institutions, there is a loss of our sense of community. We no longer enjoy the same bonds of communality of previous generations, but are far more isolated and atomised in how we live together. The bonds of marriage, family and community have withered as we increasingly see our lives as exercises in individualistic pursuits.

Once again, the loss of community finds its roots in the severance of a deeper relationship, namely the relationship with one's own life, one's own deepest desires, one's own vocation or calling. As each of us becomes seduced by the pressures of materialism and the expectation to be seen as wealthy, strong and prolific, we neglect the bonds of family and community and the deepest longings of our own hearts, which are the cornerstones of a life that is joyful. Once we are seduced from the search for our deepest dream, we no longer live our lives from a centre of inspiration, direction and purpose. Rather, we go on but not knowing why, with lives devoid of meaning, reference or connection.

The dis-integration of these relationships finds its genesis in the severance of our most profound relationship, being our relationship with God, with the One who holds us together in balance. For this is the loss of the relationship with the centre in each one of us and in the whole of creation. Once this relationship is neglected, we have no source, no reference point, no basis to protect us from the erosion of anxiety. At this point, we have lost the sense of the centre, where we can find the One who inspires us, cares for us and protects us from being scattered. Through this deterioration, we can see that this era of fragmentation marks the disintegration of four relationships, which form the cornerstone of human happiness and fulfilment.

Our experience of the breakdown of these relationships has the potential to humble us and bring us to a new awareness that we are out of touch with the centre of our lives. When we experience the pain of loneliness, meaninglessness and anxiety as commonplace in our lives, we must come to a realisation that our perception of reality and of what makes life worthwhile is profoundly distorted. Essentially, we are not in touch with *the* centre which holds our lives together and which gives everything a sense of reference, meaning and purpose. When a potter uses the wheel, the starting point is the correct placement of the clay in the centre of the wheel. Throughout the creation of the piece, the centre must be constantly honoured as the wheel revolves or else the piece loses its shape and finally disintegrates. We are now at that stage of disintegration and the clay that is our lives must be fixed again upon the centre.

In response to this condition, the contemporary challenge for the Christian faith is to articulate a vision and practice, centred upon the love of Jesus Christ, which responds to the fragmentation of these relationships. The Christian message is simply not connecting at this time because it is not being conveyed through images, concepts and symbols, which resonate with the unconscious distress in us arising from the fragmentation of these relationships. We need to re-discover the meaning and significance of the Christian vision as the way towards a new integrity that restores:

- the relationship of the individual to his or her Creator;

- the relationship of the individual to the divine calling or vocation in his or her life;

- the relationship of the individual to others in the intimacy of marriage, family and community;

- the relationship of the individual to society and to creation itself, as governed by the central institutions of law, religion and politics.

This essay is based upon the personal conviction that the integrity of the Christian faith is *the* response to the fragmentation of these relationships and that their re-integration is the need of our time.

The essence of this approach in the Christian faith is the arousal of the interior and dormant attraction within the human person to Jesus Christ. As one enters into a growing attraction to Him, one's life becomes more integrated and these central relationships become reconciled at a deeper and more profound level. So many of us are scattered by constant anxieties each day. As one begins to find the steadfast, eternal presence of the love of Jesus Christ within oneself, one becomes more concentrated and gathered together in one's daily life. This phenomenon is analogous to what occurs when one places a magnet beneath a page of scattered iron filings. Before positioning the magnet, the filings are scattered, disjointed and eccentric. When the magnet is placed in the centre, beneath the surface, they are effortlessly re-ordered in concentric circles in their attraction to this centre.

Recently, I visited Newgrange with two close friends. I was struck by how important the symbol of the spiral was to our ancestors. Over three thousand years before the incarnation of Christ, the people of this era used the stone carving of the spiral as their most sacred symbol. In each spiral, it may be that they recognised the source of life as emanating from a centre, from which all things emerge and from which all things find meaning. Perhaps their wisdom remains rooted in the depths of our unconscious, calling us to remember that our lives need reference to a divine centre.

The heart of the Christian message is that we need the centrality of Jesus Christ in order to bring shape and integrity to our own lives. His loving presence, in the centre of the human heart, is the magnetic attraction that leads to the reconciliation and at-one-ment of all relationships. If we forget this, as we have now done, these central relationships weaken and ultimately fragment. Given this contemporary context, the question now for the Christian faith is simply this: how can we develop a vision and practice of the Christian faith which re-connects us to His loving presence and in turn to our own deepest self, each other and creation itself?

In my own continuing search for an answer to this question, the most insightful writing which I have found is that of the American integral philosopher, Ken Wilber. There are two central, recurring themes in his writings. It is suggested that they could form the bedrock for a vision and practice of the Christian faith, which connects with the unconscious need of so many people for a spiritual basis to their lives, which they are not finding in the established religious practices of the Christian churches.

The first theme is that a vision and practice of the Christian faith, that will connect with the real needs of people, must follow a continuum from matter, to body, to mind, to soul, and ultimately, to Spirit. Each of these spheres in the human person must be honoured so that the Christian faith speaks to the whole human person. The second theme is that the human person has a propensity to develop in four directions. Each of us has an interior and an exterior life. Each of us also has a yearning to be an individual and yet a member of the collective. Accordingly, we yearn to develop in four directions which are:

- interior and individual;

- exterior and individual;

- interior and collective;

- exterior and collective.

Similarly, the Christian faith needs to be articulated in a way that gives purpose and meaning to the human person as one evolves in each of these directions. For to be fully alive, one must honour all of these dimensions and do so in a way that integrates matter, body, mind, soul and Spirit in each of them. If the love of Jesus Christ is to bring integrity to our lives, the Christian faith must be spoken of and practised so as to enable us to be fully alive in this way.

THE INTERIOR INDIVIDUAL LIFE

A Christian faith, which honours the interior individual life, must recognise the central importance of individual *prayer*. Prayer is the means of developing an interior relationship and ultimately, the inward, individual experience of the divine. The experience of prayer draws a person back into the centre so that a re-

integration begins and leads effortlessly to a new order and coherence.

The practice of prayer within the Christian faith, however,
needs to honour the intrinsic progression from matter, to body,
to mind, to soul and then, Spirit. The starting point is matter,
that is the choice of a suitable place for prayer and the development of that sacred space. If one is involved in the prepara-
tion of this space within one's own home or community, it will
increase the power of it as a place of prayer. One must then
honour the body and the breath. Any strain or discomfort in the
body or the breath must be attended to. If not, it will form a
constant distraction throughout the period of prayer. In turn, the
mind must be quietened or employed in a way that meets its
need, so that it enters into silence. A mantra may be used or
one may choose to reflect upon scripture.

Once all of these aspects of one's person have been attended to, the soul then comes to prominence. It is at this point
that repressed emotions and deep-seated feelings are aroused
from the unconscious and cry out to be integrated. Persistent
negative thought patterns, distorted imagery and signs of compulsive behaviour are confronted, so that the image of one's life
and oneself can be reformed in the vision that one is loved by
God. The roots of the distorted vision of oneself, which has led
to prolonged feelings of anger or anxiety, are now being cut. At
this stage, a spiritual director, that is a person who has personal, profound experience in prayer, is essential in order to
guide one through the overwhelming feelings which will inevitably arise.

In time, a new vision can then take hold, a vision of oneself
as loved by God and ultimately, as being in God, in Spirit and
in truth. This is the final stage of prayer. One does not so much
enter into this stage but rather one is drawn or invited into it.
This stage is the culmination of all prayer in that it is the entry
into the direct, arresting experience of God, as love. In these
moments of true contemplative experience, one is held in ar-
rest by the still motion of love. Here, one's whole person is
gripped by the beauty of God and by the unfathomable love
that is the light in each one of us, the full realisation of the Spirit
in the human person.

THE EXTERIOR INDIVIDUAL LIFE

In order to articulate a Christian vision and practice, which allows for the exterior, individual dimension of human life, we must also recognise the importance of *discernment*. In general, discernment is the means by which we become sensitive to the movement of the Spirit in our lives. It enables us to appreciate experiences in our lives as moments of profound revelation of the love of God for us. In reflecting upon these experiences, we can discern the message being revealed to each one of us, which is that we are loved by God and loved uniquely.

A more specific understanding of the gift of discernment is that which enables us to see the choices with which we are faced and to see which option leads to happiness. The key to discernment in this sense is that one seeks to make the choice which is grounded in the principle and foundation of the love of God. Discernment calls for reflection on the choices with which one is presented so that one follows what is simply being set before one by God rather than one's own unreal expectations or those of others. The dynamics of discernment, which were articulated by St Ignatius of Loyola in the *Spiritual Exercises*, are quite simply a fifth gospel and the unexplored treasure of our Christian heritage.

In order to discern the true calling in one's life, it is essential to undergo that process with the assistance of a spiritual director or mentor. In honouring the desire for vocation, one senses a point of departure. At this point, one has to have the courage to look beyond the accepted conditioning of one's peers and truly seek the unique, individual calling for one's own life. As one is then going into unchartered waters, the guidance of a spiritual director or a mentor helps one to detect the movement of the Spirit and to foster the strength and fortitude to follow this calling.

One is then called into a phase of initiation which leads to a point of completely surrendering one's life and actions to a higher purpose, a greater ideal, a cause larger than oneself. Ultimately, one is led into a spirit of openness and surrender to God. One surrenders to the quiet unfolding of God's plan amid the limitations of human poverty, so that one is transfigured by the love of God.

The final stage of discernment is the point of return. When one is initiated, one is called to return to the place from which one has left and to bring back to it the vision that was missing and which has been found. When Jesus was transfigured, He faced toward Jerusalem, to the place where He would return to fully reveal His message, the complete and total love of God. True contemplative experience translates into return to the world, contemplation in action, for the real contemplative is not running away from the world but tries to act in the world at a deeper level.

THE INTERIOR COLLECTIVE LIFE

The Christian faith has always espoused the general principle that the necessary milieu for prayer and discernment is *community* with others. The interior communal life provides essential support and encouragement in being attentive to one's personal relationship with God and in finding a source of reference for the active discernment of vocation which will ensue. The spiritual journey requires companionship.

What the Christian faith has neglected, however, at an enormous cost, is that true community must be based upon the human desire for intimacy. Where there is no intimacy, there is no community. Where there is no intimacy among people who say they are in a community, people will not join that community and it will wither and die. More significantly, with the primary model for Christian communities being based on celibacy as opposed to marriage, the Christian tradition has tended to denigrate marriage and family life as a crucible for finding one's own authentic experience of Christ. Yet, the growth of intimacy with a significant person in our lives nurtures the search for Christ in our lives. The development of a loving relationship with that person arouses the dormant conviction in our unconscious of His love. In human intimacy with another, we catch glimpses of the depth of God's love for us.

When the desire for intimacy leads to a conscious commitment between two persons, the most sustainable basis for community takes root and becomes embodied through them. After one makes this commitment to another, the relationship naturally expands to embrace others. The bedrock is in place for familial and communal relationships to develop and thrive. We are now being called to re-appraise Christian community as a natural evolution of marriage and family life. This form of community would evolve from a maturing of relationships based on familial ties to those based on mutual recognition of the inner relationship with Christ.

Such an approach would mark a significant departure from the traditional understanding of Christian community as being a matter for religious orders, based on the practice of celibacy. The understanding of Christian community as the natural progression of marriage and family life, has not found true expression in the structures of "parishes" or "local communities" either. Such communities draw from an identity based on geographical location, economic ties and communal endeavours, rather than a shared spiritual identity. Rather, a true Christian community is marked by a committed relationship between people whose common bond is their inner attraction to the vision of Jesus Christ. The development of communities based on this identity marks the full flourishment of Christian marriage and family life and remains relatively unexplored.

THE EXTERIOR COLLECTIVE LIFE

The true test as to whether a Christian vision and practice of prayer, discernment and community are authentic is whether they lead to *justice* in our society. The term "justice" is used here to mean the restoration of right relationship. This can take the form of justice in the workings of society, social justice, and also ecological justice, which refers to the restoration of right relationship between the human person and the environment.

The desire for justice in the human person is the hallmark of an inner life which is flourishing. Ultimately, contemplation leads into compassion for others, particularly for those who are un-represented and marginalised by society and a greater sensitivity to nature and creation. In honouring relationships in community, one also becomes conscious of the need to work for the concerns of an ever-widening community. One is propelled into the concerns of social and ecological justice.

This desire for social and ecological justice can only be realised through a new vision of the purpose of the social institutions which form the structure of society. Western society is held together by the institutions of three essential systems, which determine the quality of justice, being the legal, religious and political systems. A Christian vision of our exterior collective life must look to the institutions provided by these systems and stand for an approach rooted in the transcendent in each of them. It is only when a transcendent vision takes hold of these institutions that justice will flourish in our society.

The first institution which needs to find an anchor in the transcendent, is the legal system, being the place in society to which the individual has initial recourse in relation to an issue of justice in their life. It is in the legal system that the divine ideal of justice is meant to be realised. The discovery of a transcendent anchor in the legal system will lead to the fostering to two mutually supporting objectives, namely the development of an ethos of public service among those who practise in the administration of this system and the pursuit of greater access to justice in the workings of the legal system.

It is ironic to suggest that religious institutions need to rediscover a transcendent anchor. The institutions of Christianity have, however, declined greatly by placing a false God, namely the clerical power of these institutions, before the honouring of the movement of the Spirit. Once the centrality of Christ is displaced, fragmentation has occurred in relationships which are critical to a true vision of Christ. The Church must become the place where we find new thinking and a new commitment in the soul of our society to integrity, arising from the recognition of our unity in Christ and our diversity as agents for the kingdom of God. The role of the Church is therefore to draw upon the personal experience of its members and to articulate with humility and yet boldness, the *paradiso*, the true life, the full flourishment of human goodness and endeavour.

The final stage in the quest for justice is found in a renewal of the political system, being the working out of the vision of the kingdom in the society in which we live. The political system has also suffered greatly because it has not been employed as an agent of a greater vision. Without being a servant of a greater vision, only self-interest and widespread cynicism can prevail. If the political system honours a vision of Christ, which is articulated and protected by the institutions of the Christian faith, it can draw from the soul of society and work out the ideal that we are all members of one body and that one body is uniquely present in each one of us. This is a vision of integrated citizenship. In so doing, the political system will fulfil its potential as the place where the kingdom of God is made real and revealed in all of its glory through compassion and justice.

INTEGRITAS — A CENTRE FOR THE DEVELOPMENT OF AN INTEGRAL APPROACH TO THE CHRISTIAN FAITH

In a family home in Stoneyford, County Kilkenny, a small experiment entitled "Integritas" is being attempted by a group of people in which the central elements of an integral Christian vision and practice — prayer, discernment, community and justice — are being followed in some simple ways. On the first and third Wednesday evenings of each month, Christian meditation and contemplative prayer is held in a room designed for this practice. Throughout the year, a number of day and evening courses are arranged in the hope that a school in prayer and discernment will emerge. The primary purpose of these courses is to provide spiritual guidance and the enhancement of discernment for those who are present for the evenings of Christian meditation and contemplative prayer.

These two ventures are being undertaken there within the context of a family home. The house was designed to cater for a family and yet also act as a place for prayer. The purpose behind this is to articulate that prayer and reflection can take root within the context of the intimacy of marriage and family life. They are not exclusive of each other but rather mutually supportive.

The ultimate aim of this is the emergence of an integral Christian vision and practice in due time, based upon the experience and consensus of people who come there. The practice of Christian meditation and contemplative prayer and the development of a school in prayer and discernment, within the context of a family home, will hopefully provide the milieu for this vision to be developed, renewed and re-defined.

At the end of each of the evenings there, the prayer recited below is read. It draws together the central conviction that by being committed to the practice of prayer, discernment, community and justice, the Christian faith can lead to the re-integration of the central relationships in our lives. Ultimately, if the love of Jesus Christ is at the centre, a sense of lasting integrity will develop in our lives in which we will become at one with God, with ourselves, with each other and with creation. By abiding in His love for us, we will come to be at One.

> May we enable each other to trust entirely
> in the provident love of God;
> may we form family, community and a deeper identity
> in the gentle attraction of Jesus Christ;
> may we support one another in responding to the unique
> call of the Spirit,
> and serve as one in realising the dream of the Spirit for all;
> so that in this covenant,
> may we remain in Christ,
> and with Christ in each of us,
> may we come to be at One.

Chapter 10

FAITH, PHILOSOPHY AND TRUST

Patrick Quinn

INTRODUCTION

My own interest (though perhaps that is too mild or neutral a word) in the areas of faith and reason and the connections between them is both personal and academic. I was born into a traditional Irish Catholic family, studied philosophy at undergraduate and post-graduate level with postgraduate studies in theology, and have published in and taught courses on philosophy, including the philosophy of religion, at college and university level. Within that context and the timespan involved, there have been various adjustments made in my own understanding of faith and of philosophy and in my views about how the two are related. As a result, there have been some interesting shifts in my thinking over the years.

Looking back from the perspective of the present, I can say with certainty that I do consider myself fortunate to have been given the gift of faith in the context of having been brought up in the Catholic tradition with the kind of parents for whom Christian Catholicism was important. While there have been many times right up to the present when I have experienced immense frustration, disappointment and often deep anger with church teachings and behaviour, this has not fundamentally changed my mind about the rightness of the Catholic faith. It does sadden me at times to think that the faith which was (and

still is to quite an extent) so much a part of Irish life, is now increasingly dismissed and often rejected almost quite casually
by more and more Irish people, especially the young. Such a
response, I think, prevents the richness of Christianity being
appreciated and valued for what it is and for what it can provide
for individuals and for society generally. It also devalues the
efforts of so many generations of Irish women and men who historically tried to sustain and transmit the faith often in a climate
of very great difficulties and persecution and in the face of
threats to human life itself. I do think that we live in an Ireland
now that is characterised by very brash forms of materialism
with a very public and unapologetic emphasis on individualism.
This seems to be almost all-pervasive and results in a value system which is quite dominant in contemporary Irish life. This is
an era of a "bread and circuses" mentality and one of the results too often is an ethical vacuum where the sense of what is
morally right and wrong is blunted or silenced.

AN UNDERSTANDABLE RESPONSE

The social and individual rejection of the importance of Irish
Catholicism by those brought up in that tradition is in many
ways understandable. It is undoubtedly a reaction to the ecclesiastical authoritarianism of the past (and present), especially in
the area of sexuality, and to the flawed and often hypocritical
approach of the clerical Church towards the need for justice
and truth. The perception is strong that a form of clerical pro-
tectionism and patronage operates for offending clerics, especially in the area of the sexual abuse of the young. This has
been and continues to be a major public source of scandal in
Ireland and has greatly undermined the credibility of the
church itself and the message it proclaims with particularly dis-
astrous effects on the faith of young people. There are, of
course, other factors which have contributed to the new almost
post-Christian society that now exists in Ireland. These include
the breakdown of family life, the growing increase in violence
generally (particularly violence for its own sake) and, not least
of all, the surge in material wealth, especially since the early
1990s. It is also true to say that fame, pleasure and wealth now

seem to define the central aspirations for a growing number of people in Ireland.

What is interesting, I find, is that many students of philosophy in the colleges in which I teach, often seem to see in the subject the opportunity to explore their own beliefs or lack of them in a more objective and probing way. I would be quite aware of this as a lecturer in philosophy. Students are indeed, from this point of view, working on themselves, as the famous philosopher Ludwig Wittgenstein (1889-1951) put it[1] when they explore and analyse theological aspects of reality from a philosophical point of view. How general this is, I wouldn't know, though I suspect it is reasonably widespread given the nature of philosophical studies in themselves and the close ties which philosophy and religion have always had, especially in the case of the relationship between Christianity and Greek philosophy in the Western tradition of thought. As someone who teaches philosophy, I have also had the opportunity within that discipline to explore the connections between philosophy and the Christian faith to which I subscribe and the exchanges which I've had with students in the course of various lectures over the years have often been enormously helpful to me in straightening out my own ideas on these subjects.

THE ISSUE OF CREDIBILITY

From the late 1960s onwards, it became increasingly obvious to me as to others whom I knew that the Catholic Church had some very serious issues to address in terms of its clerical and hierarchical perception of Church authority, specifically with regards to the whole area of human sexuality. This was highlighted by the Papal Encyclical of 1968, *Humanae Vitae*. One of the most momentous church events that took place during the early 1960s was the Second Vatican Council (1962–1965), which was a radical attempt by the great Pope John XXIII to renew the Church in very significant and fundamental ways so as to make it more inclusive and accessible for all both internally and externally. Little mention is made now of this great churchman (a sign of the present times, no doubt) and Vatican II itself seems to have been in many important ways forgotten. Yet this "caretaker" and "peasant" pope, despite his harmless and benign appearance, was a radical facilitator of change and a fundamentally humble man who had an innate understanding of what Church leadership really meant. He had an instinct for the ordinary and initiated on an official ecclesiastical level a new concern for openness in the Church with implications for changes within it and in its external relationships. There was a new feeling of excitement then that a fresh start could be made though this obviously brought its own fears to those in the clerical hierarchy who were cautious and resistant to change. Even after death of this great Pope in 1963, the effects of his original vision for renewal continued and were carried through as much as possible by his successor, Pope Paul VI, during the Council and there was a growing sense that Catholics could now practise their faith in a more mature and inclusive way.

The crisis came, however, with the publication of Pope Paul's Papal Encyclical *Humanae Vitae* in 1968 which forbade what was then described as artificial contraception (i.e. any methods such as the Pill, then recently available). The recommended approach was for natural family planning methods where sexual intercourse was regulated in relation to the woman's reproductive cycle. The impact of this encyclical was to have a catastrophic effect on the Church's credibility and authority, especially with regards to issues of sexuality, and more indirectly on people's general perception of Vatican II. The whole area of family planning was undoubtedly a contentious one and Pope Paul did set up a commission of clerical and non-clerical specialists to examine the issues involved. What was interesting was that, although at the start, many of the commission members were not in favour of artificial contraception, as time went on their views changed with the result that most eventually did support the possibility of artificial contraception family planning methods as well as those described as natural. Unfortunately, the Pope did not take this into account and the result was a Papal Encyclical that was divisive and confusing in its teachings and which lacked credibility for many theologians, priests and religious, and for many Catholics worldwide. It was clear to many people that there was a serious credibility gap and this raised questions about the church's authority, specifically in the area of human sexuality. The fallout was dramatic at times though often more quietly subversive as in Ireland.

Ireland, like the rest of the Western world and the US was also changing in the 1960s, if more slowly, particularly economically and socially and towards the end of the decade, politically. However, the Catholic faith was still very important and widely regarded here as a fundamental bedrock that grounded the Irish way of life. However, to what extent the Vatican Council impinged on Irish people is difficult to assess. Certainly, knowledge about what it meant was not actively encouraged at ecclesiastical level most of all in Dublin where Archbishop McQuaid on returning from Rome famously had announced that nothing had changed. There were of course some like Father Austin Flannery and Sean MacReamoinn who tried to convey the importance of the Council to Irish people but by and large it seems that Vatican II as a significant Christian event in many ways passed Ireland by apart from some liturgical changes. What did have a more lasting and public effect on Irish life was the whole debate that surrounded the issue of artificial contraception and this ultimately led many here to use their own discretion about what family planning methods they would accept, artificial or otherwise. This was to have long-term consequences on Irish church life on issues of sexuality and later resulted in public and bitter disputes about abortion and divorce, which some people contrived to associate with the issue of contraception. Many, however, simply went ahead and made their own decisions and this implicitly undermined church credibility in relation to at least some issues on authority, notably in the field of human sexuality.

The hopes that Vatican II raised and the subsequent debates about contraception led me to ask questions about church credibility and power. At the time during these events I was strongly convinced that the Church's stance on the whole contraception debate was mistaken and unfortunate and I have had no reason to change my views over the years. The nature of the discussions at ecclesiastical level and the decisions taken certainly raised for me and for others very serious problems about church authority and in its approach particularly to human sexuality. I have sometimes wondered whether the rather obsessive and oppressive focus on sexuality by the church and the clerical hierarchy is an interest that results from the lifestyle and attitudes that would seem to characterise an unmarried male priesthood with the lack of relevant experience and a certain immaturity of knowledge about the reality of human sexual relationships that is associated with that. I did come to accept, however, that the church does make serious mistakes (it has done so historically on a whole range of significant areas) and I learned that one needs to be personally judicious about deciding what is acceptable in the church's teachings and approach and what is not. My perceptions of church authority, including its specific views on human sexuality, did without doubt affect the way in which I subsequently came to see the church so that while I continued to have faith in the Christian message I was much more careful to think through the implications of church teaching and its recommendations and to cultivate for myself a much more critical faith.

PHILOSOPHY

Teaching philosophy and thinking through my philosophical views subsequently gave me a welcome opportunity to examine my beliefs in a critical way and to view my religious attitudes from a speculative distance in the light of the kind of issues outlined above. My reading on various aspects of philosophical thought and the opportunities which were made available to me to think through my beliefs from a more considered philosophical and somewhat detached perspective did provide me in an ongoing way with the chance to try to straighten out my own thinking about faith and the relationship between faith and reason. The interplay between what we believe and our attempts to critically evaluate our beliefs is complex and life-long for those interested in allowing themselves to think about such issues and, to my mind, there is no easy resolution to the faith-reason debate. What I like about philosophy is that it enables a person to take a distance and assume an objectivity about religion which I'm not sure is that easy to do from an exclusively theological point of view. There is a great sense of freedom in philosophically speculating about God and religious issues and this is also what undoubtedly appeals to students of philosophy who want to explore their own religious viewpoints and conclusions. However, faith is also a commitment (Wittgenstein describes it as a passionate commitment to a system of reference)[2] and there are many times in life when one has to come in from the sidelines and become actively engaged with what one claims to believe. In my own case, I have come to realise that philosophical thinking on its own would never be sufficient to convince me personally that my beliefs are correct. I cannot as it were reason myself into believing but instead always start out from a position of belief and, in that context, explore and understand what I can of the implications and basis of what my beliefs amount to, in so far as that is possible to do. Just as philosophy can sometimes put before us in a clear way what we have always implicitly known, so too can religious faith enable us to see the world through our beliefs in a particularly convincing and believing way. Seeing the world from the latter perspective (as from others) is of course tested as one goes through life, especially in the very difficult times which all of us experience or will eventually come to experience at some point. Faith can then be reduced to its essence — a simple straightforward non-intellectual acceptance of and commitment to God which in the case of Christians means to God made human in Jesus, Who is believed to be there for us in our time of need. This is very different to the kind of speculative approach that one can adopt at other times when life is going well for us, for example, or when we think about God or religion in a philosophical way. In that sense, the God of human speculation and the God of human need are understood and appreciated very differently and even seem to inhabit different levels of reality, as far as human consciousness is concerned.

OTHER BENEFITS OF PHILOSOPHY

Philosophy can also help in telling us something about God. Perhaps the most significant and paradoxical example of this which would have impressed me concerns how little we can in fact know about God. This is one of the remarkable contributions of St Thomas Aquinas to the debate on faith and reason. In Book 1 of his famous text, *Summa Contra Gentiles*, Aquinas spends a number of chapters telling us what God is not and he concludes by declaring that God is uniquely one and simple. Knowing that we do not know God is a remarkable insight to my mind and one that proves useful from the point of view of faith. This conclusion was also stated by other thinkers, notably the medieval Jewish philosopher, Moses Maimonides, and its roots can be traced, at least in Western thinking, back to the Platonic Socrates who insisted that knowledge of our own ignorance is a necessary prerequisite for cultivating the right disposition for wisdom.

On the other hand, the various proofs for the existence of God that are found in the history of philosophy are not very convincing to me nor personally persuasive. While they may from a philosophical point of view represent clever and often intricate arguments which have a certain intellectual appeal, from the point of view of convincing anyone that God exists, that is something else altogether. The general underlying claim that many of these arguments make in demonstrating that there must be a supreme absolute being is one with which I can agree but the value of many of these arguments or proofs for me lie in their ability to show us ways of thinking about God (as unchanging, uncaused, supremely perfect, ultimate Lawgiver, omniscient, all-powerful). None that I have read to date are persuasive enough for me to accept the existence of God on the basis of those arguments alone.

There is an interesting point here about how far reason and faith interpenetrate each other and Kant, the eighteenth century German philosopher, has made some valid remarks about this.[3] He argued that there must be flexibility for those who investigate theological issues from a scholarly point of view and he gives the example of the pastor who when preaching follows the relevant orthodox church doctrines but when involved in philosophical-theological enquiries is entitled to explore these much more freely. This raises questions not only for scholars but also for all believers, i.e. how far does one go in critically thinking about one's beliefs? Where is the cutoff point? What criteria should be used to rationally check one's beliefs? Should philosophical or scientific thinking be the arbiter of one's religious beliefs and of religious truth?

CORRECT BELIEF AND TRUST

My own view is that it is difficult if not impossible to be wholly neutral and to assume an impersonal and clinical objective distance with regards to how we judge our religious beliefs or lack of them. Towards the end of Plato's dialogue, *Theaetetus*, Socrates provides a very interesting definition of knowledge as correct belief. Following on from this, I think that all of us are necessarily believing human beings from the very outset. We accept on trust a world view, a way of seeing our environment, locally and globally, from our parents and other relatives, our teachers and other significant adults, our culture, society, historical place in time and from the whole cluster of socio-political and individual influences that shape our ways of being with one another. We start out with a basic belief system, which includes an acceptance or rejection of or an indifference to a religious way of seeing the world. Of course, we can and do change our way of seeing the world but even if we reject our original ways of belief and trust, we still replace them with other beliefs and with other forms of trust. For example, there are unfortunately those who because of the abuse of their trust, learn not to trust people except perhaps under certain strict conditions. Here, the belief that people can be trusted is replaced by a belief that certain (perhaps most) people cannot be trusted. Belief is part of what we are as human beings and religious belief is part of that condition. To my mind, therefore, it is always from the perspective of some belief system to which we adhere (e.g. that God exists generally or in some defined way, as in the Christian God, or that God does not exist at all, or that we choose to remain agnostic about whether God exists or not) that we come to examine critically any notions about belief. Belief and faith is ultimately about a personal commitment to trust in the rightness of what one believes or has faith in. The history of religious faith contains many examples of extraordinary persons who were trusted to represent, personify and transmit the essence of various religious beliefs such as Moses, Jesus, Mohammed, the Buddha and others. The question arises though as to how anyone can ever be certain about the correctness of his or her beliefs.

This, interestingly enough, is a question about the nature of knowledge itself and is frequently discussed in philosophy. It seems to me that the very nature of knowledge requires us to accept that to acquire any knowledge in the first place, we are put in the position of having to initially accept what is unprovable. As children, we trust in our parents and teachers, for example, to tell us what is true. That is the basis for learning. Knowledge is acquired in the context of belief and trust and if we later discover through experience and/or critical thinking, that some of what we were told was untrue, we then adjust our views accordingly though we remain in the condition where we must still trust someone or something in order to acquire further knowledge. The catastrophe is that some people as children learn that their parents and/or teachers are not to be trusted and develop subsequent beliefs about the untrustworthiness of those in authority.[4] This is the scandal of corrupting the young — abusing the trusting openness of the child. The point is, I think, to acknowledge that whatever objective certainty we get in life about anything, can only come about in whatever context of belief and trust which we inhabit. On a more positive note, the kind of belief and trust that is fortunately well-grounded do provide us with rich insights into the goodness of life and this is where one can be thankful for having been given a personal and social context which intrinsically contained and contributes to the rightness of one's beliefs and to a positive and enhanced way of life as a result. Even at a minimal level, where belief and trust was abused, truth, no matter how painful, can be found.

Faith and belief (and not necessarily meaning religious faith) but most of all trust (as trusting in people), as I have suggested here, are basic to all our knowledge of whatever kind, and to life itself. This is what grounds reason. How we proceed from that towards a questioning and critical faith is a complex journey. If our reasoning leads us to the conclusion that our initial position on faith and belief is no longer to be relied upon, then, as was mentioned earlier, we still cannot opt out of assuming another set of beliefs in which we then come to trust, no matter how tentatively.

There are critical life experiences in which we do have to commit ourselves in trust to other people in whom we decide (or may be compelled) to have faith. If we are seriously ill, we trust that the doctors and nurses who look after us will do their best to help us. On a more immediate level, there are those with whom we are immediately linked, our families, spouses, partners, children, parents, other relatives, friends whom we trust, especially perhaps in times of personal crisis. Trust is seen as particularly necessary at critical times and we do not generally sit around speculating for too long during such periods but commit ourselves immediately to the trust of those whom we believe can help us.

It strikes me that trust is so fundamental to human life and often so hidden when times are good, that it really only shows its true character when we are up against serious, even life-threatening, personal experiences. It is this perspective which I think must fundamentally inform our search for knowledge including for the kind of certainties which we would like to have at least about the important issues in life. I am reminded of the preamble by the medieval churchman and logician, St Anselm, who was convinced that the reality of God's existence could be accepted on the basis of a unique definition of God as a being than whom nothing greater can be conceived.[5] Anselm claimed that he did not seek to understand in order to believe but that he was convinced that unless he believed, he should not be able to understand. If belief and faith, as I have suggested here, really amount to trust, then the debate on faith and philosophy becomes a debate about how much we can trust in our fundamental beliefs about human life and the world in which we live, and crucially, about how much we can trust in rational analysis and in our reasoning powers to show us what is true. Since belief in reason is by definition a belief in our intelligence to enable us to discover whether our beliefs are true, faith in reason itself is also at issue here. The point is that whether we like it or not, our thinking (including our belief-thinking) will always exist in this kind of circularity where our need for fundamental beliefs of some kind as a basis for any kind of thinking can elude any impersonal clinical attempts to assess them critically. Of course, our ability to abstract and intellectually distil what we consider to be the salient points of the issues that we consider is a guarantee of objectivity. Nevertheless, if the context of such abstraction, as it must be, is that of a belief system in which we fundamentally trust, irrespective of its nature, then belief in the power of reason is itself subject to the kind of circularity mentioned above.

What all this seems to come down to is that if we want to find ourselves in a position where we can acquire true and certain knowledge, especially about the most important aspects of human life, then we need to be fortunate enough to be committed to the right kind of belief system in order to guarantee access. Those with strong religious beliefs, for example, are convinced and trust in the respective creeds to which they subscribe, as do those who operate out of secular cultures of conviction also. In a very real sense, no one can stand on the sidelines and spend much time wondering and speculating about their faith as the basis of action, as was said already. Instead people act (often react) out of their respective systems of beliefs, often with a passionate if sometimes implicit commitment to them, to find out what is necessary. It is in this context that religious faith is seen as a gift and the disposition for such faith is believed to have its origin outside the natural world i.e. as grace. What is interesting about Wittgenstein, the philosopher mentioned earlier, is that while he was a man who was fascinated by religion, notably Christianity and specifically Catholicism, and described many of its features very insightfully indeed, he gives the impression of someone who stands on the sidelines as an onlooker, like a spectator watching a game, who cannot find in himself sufficient reason or motivation to participate in the play. By contrast, the French philosopher Gabriel Marcel, who adopted an ongoing reflective approach to reality as mystery, was moved to commit himself from a purely philosophical way of considering life towards an explicit commitment to Christian conversion as a Catholic.[6] In their different ways, their writings and lifestyles represent the speculative philosophical approach to faith as in the case of Wittgenstein, and the passionate trusting commitment to faith in Christianity which marked the life of Marcel. In religious terms, this might be explained as the mystery of grace which shows itself in the personal disposition of some but not in others.

PHILOSOPHY, FAITH AND TRUTH

Philosophy in the best sense of the term and religious faith aim to find truth, that is, to see reality as it is. Unfortunately, although truth is the declared goal of church teaching, primarily the truth about God, far too often it has been the case that concern for the truth is not always personified in the Catholic Church at an ecclesiastical and hierarchical level. This, of course, once again raises serious questions of credibility. Concealing or refusing to debate the truth (e.g. as in issues concerning sexual abuse or allowing access by women to the priesthood) is wrong and leads increasingly to a failure of courage on the part of clerical representatives of the church as an institution to address the truth of other issues also (such as ethics in business life, national and international aggression etc.).

To return to a point made at the beginning of this piece: the openness that was heralded by Vatican II was never more desirable than in the present time. The debate on the relationship between philosophy (and other kinds of analytical and scientific thinking) and faith is one that will undoubtedly continue. It has been suggested that knowledge of whatever kind aims at showing us ways of seeing the world and how we are in it. This is the point of philosophical discussion in that the arguments presented are really saying: *look at things this way*! Like philosophy, religious faith also shows us a way of seeing the world which it is argued is fundamental and essential to our human well-being. Whether we subscribe to that or not, we still cannot escape from trusting in certain ways of seeing the world which may be true or false or partly true or partly false. We will be fortunate indeed if we are given a form of understanding which allows us to see as much as possible about reality as it is and it is the conviction of religious believers that this is possible from their respective faiths. The question arises, of course, as to what is the true faith. Religious believers hope and trust and are convinced that their respective faith is just that. It is like the activity of climbing a mountain. Each climber hopes to get to the top. Achieving that goal will vary depending on each person and on his or her circumstances, i.e. whether the pace of travel is faster or slower, the point of departure from which each begins, the rests taken along the way and so on. What is essential to have is a conscientious desire to reach the top, to trust that this is possible and to make whatever efforts one can to achieve that in the belief that there is a worthwhile end to such efforts. A different kind of metaphor is supplied by Wittgenstein on the subject of religion, though it might also usefully serve as a metaphor for a strong faith:

> Religion is, as it were, the calm bottom of the sea at its deepest point, which remains calm however high the waves on the surface may be. (*Culture and Value*, 53e)

Notes

[1] *Culture and Value* by Ludwig Wittgenstein ed. G.H. Von Wright in collaboration with Heikke Nyman, trans. Peter Winch, Basil Blackwell, Oxford, 1980, p.16e.

[2] *Ibid.* 64e.

[3] See Kant's essay: *Answer to the Question: What is Enlightenment?* in *Basic Writings of Kant* ed. Allen W. Wood, Modern Library, Random House Inc., New York, 2001, pp.133–141.

[4] For an interesting account of trust, see *A Question of Trust* by Onora O'Neill, Cambridge University Press, Cambridge, 2002.

[5] This is known as the Ontological Argument reproduced in *The Ontological Argument* ed. Alvin Plantinga, Macmillan, London, 1968, p.3 *et seq.*

[6] See *The Philosophy of Existence* by Gabriel Marcel, trans. Manya Harari, The Harvill Press, London, 1948, pp.1-31. Also *The Mystery of Being* Vols. I & II, by Gabriel Marcel, Gateway Editions, South Bend, Indiana, 1950/51.